Praise for the Book . . .

Sumalatha Vasudeva has been a beloved friend of mine all along. A thorough professional, visionary and a worthy contemporary to note, she has been actively involved in child, adolescent and geriatric sciences and her work demonstrates her vast knowledge and experience in these fields. Through her book she has brought out in detail the dilemmas and emotional ups and downs experienced by many. The methods to preserve mental health and bring about inner peace, advocated by her, are simple and straightforward. It is common knowledge that she in all these years has dedicated herself totally to her profession. Even while helping many, she has sought to serve society at large by her creative and academic pursuits.

I sincerely urge one and all to purchase this book and be benefitted by it. The outreach of this book would be the deserving moral success that Ms. Sumalatha Vasudeva deserves. Once again congratulations to Sumalatha Vasudeva for investing her heart and soul in this creative endeavor.

With best wishes

Dr. Somashekar. A.R.

Professor & HOD of Pediatrics, Ramaiah Medical College Paediatric Pulmonologist and Adolescent Care Specialist, Secretary IAP State Allergy Chapter 2021, EB Central IAP- 2015 & 2017, EB.Central IAP Respiratory chapter Secretary AHA: 2016-2017, Joint Secretary IAP, Bangalore-2016, President IAP State Respiratory Chapter. 2015-2016, Treasurer: IAP Allergy chapter 2015, Chief Editor – Pulmo Scan, Executive Editor – Journal of Paediatric Pulmonology.

This book is comprehensive with topics that cover the essence of common mental disorders and the importance of mental health in one's well-being. Issues that are very relevant to our times such as stress, the influence of social media, importance of relationships within a family and with peers, importance of self-esteem and the role of academics have been covered in great detail. There is a good flow of inter-related topics that makes reading comfortable and interesting. Individuals in the field of mental health, as well as lay readers would benefit from giving this book a thorough read.

Dr. Lakshmi V. Pandit
MBBS, DPM, DNB
Consultant Psychiatrist
Bengaluru.

Think Right

108 Q & A on Mental Health

Sumalatha Vasudeva

An Imprint of Prism Books Pvt.Ltd
• Bengaluru • Chennai • Hyderabad • Kochi

Think Right

by Sumalatha Vasudeva

Published by:

Darpan An Imprint of Prism Books Pvt.Ltd

1865, 32nd Cross, 10th Main

BSK II Stage, Bengaluru 560 070, India.

Phone : 080-26714108

E-mail : logistics@prismbooks.com

Website : https://www.prismbooks.com

Also at:

Chennai : 044-24311266 Email: prismchennai@prismbooks.com

Hyderabad : 040-27612938 Email: prismhyderabad@prismbooks.com

Kochi : 0484-4000945 Email : prismkochi@prismbooks.com

First Print : 2022

Book Size : 14 cms X 21.5 cms

Paper : 70gsm NS Highbulk

Pages : XII + 112

ISBN : 978-93-91841-35-5

Layout &

Cover Design : Santosh Sheelavant

Printed at : Aditya Printers - Bengaluru

Foreword

This book deals with a wide range of mental health issues faced by people of all age groups, with special relevance to trending issues like social media addiction and the post lockdown scenarios, which have left so many people jobless, businesses defunct and families split wide apart psychologically. It answers the most common, but unanswered questions of individuals, left bewildered by the current scenario.

The reader will learn how all emotional challenges are self-perpetuated by our own reactions to certain situations and by the thoughts we then allow our minds to dwell on. This insight helps puts the power back in your court, as Sumalatha Vasudeva shows you step-by-step, how to regain a renewed sense of equanimity.

The book is a handy guide that will help you find simple solutions for complex issues. The main intention and purpose of the book is to reach as many individuals as possible in both urban and rural settings, in order to create mental health awareness, overcome stigmas, deal with stressful situations and enable people to seek help in a timely fashion.

This book offers significant help for people in low-resource settings where trained mental health professionals aren't so easily available. The author offers deep insights into the human psyche and points the reader toward making the important decision to take full responsibility for their own mental health, armed with the spiritual knowledge that each one of us creates our own reality with our own mind. A practical book for both lay and professionals alike, Sumalatha Vasudeva's wisdom radiates right to the heart of the matter.

Dr. Paula Horan
PhD (Psychology)
Reiki Master (25 years)
Won Inner Flame Award from former
Prime Minister of India (Mr. I.K. Gujral)
Best-selling author of 4 books on Reiki, 3 books on
Non-dual awareness & 1 book on Ozone Therapy

Preface

It's a given fact that most of us love wearing dazzling clothes and accessories with brand names. Using branded things in our day-to-day life seems to give us the user, a sense of chic and a cause to be recognized as one with class, appeal and higher standards. But, a large number of us do not transfer that 'Concept of Quality' to our 'Thoughts', 'Actions' and ultimately to our 'Behaviour' (as in ancient lore: Manasa – Vaacha – Karmana). This is because, the power of thought is not given due cognizance. The 'Mind' is never quiet and still at any given moment as it is constantly engaged in multiple thoughts. 'Thought' is the basis of everything we feel and ultimately how we behave.

The immense power of thought, if harnessed in an appropriate manner, can ultimately lead to a massive transformation of a person or a group. The 'Law of Attraction' also works on the 'Power of Thought'. The magic of this power is intrinsic and this immense power has to be consciously channelized for the betterment of the individual Self. Once selves are bettered, Society tends to get better and better and better.

Being a psychologist, for the last 12 years or so, I have come across a common trait among family and friends. Each one of them has a number of questions regarding mental health for which they want clear, complete and comprehensible answers and that too in person and in utmost confidentiality. There is stigma and fear of being labeled as "mentally ill" by a majority of people and sadly so by even persons having a higher level of education and sophisticated background. A majority of persons that I have personally come across are in dire need of professional help. Trapped in a vicious cycle of stigma and fear, they warily endure their circumstance and fail to disclose their problems for a long, long time. Issues which can be addressed at an early stage, with simple solutions end up coming to light after getting very, very complicated. Despite the information overload in today's world, there is lack of awareness about mental health issues and its impact on the quality of life. The basic purpose of this humble endeavour is to share the right information, create awareness about mental health issues and point out simple, yet effective ways and means to deal with them. This book has answers to 108 common queries pertaining to mental health. The easy-to-practice suggestions mentioned in the book will also help those people in settings where there is a dearth of professional intervention. Inculcating these corrective measures appropriately will definitely improve the mental health condition of an individual and prevent it from deteriorating.

This book is intended for the general public at large and especially for individuals with mental health issues and their caregivers. It will act as their companion and mentor them in dealing with specific mental health conditions. Parents and teachers can benefit from the various topics discussed in the book, to tackle head on certain issues with utmost ease. Mental health professionals too can benefit from the knowledge shared and can consider adopting the suggestions explained therein. It is my fervent belief that students and practicing psychologists will find this book useful academically and professionally.

Sumalatha Vasudeva
Psychologist

Acknowledgements

A creative work successfully accomplished without many obstacles is indeed a grace and blessing from the Almighty. I would like to express my immense gratitude to the Almighty for choosing me in particular to accomplish this task. I strongly believe that I just held the pen and it was Maa Sharada who held my hand and guided me through and through. My pranaams go to Swami Smaranandaji Maharaj, President of Ramakrishna Math and Ramakrishna Mission.

I humbly bow down and offer salutations to the revered Babuji Maharaj for his continuous blessings and guidance. I sincerely acknowledge the support garnered from the divine life force energy (Reiki) at every given moment.

I am extremely thankful to Dr. Paula Horan for devoting time to review the book and for her precious guidance. I thank Dr. Somashekhar and Dr. Lakshmi Pandit for reviewing the book. I thank Dr.Raghu K for encouraging.

It is very important with whom one shares one's dreams. I always feel I shared my dream with the right person and it is Dr. Sumana Yelluru. All along Sumana has been someone to lean on and a strong and reliable ally in helping me manifest my ardent wish. I thank you with all my heart for the support, love and encouragement.

I would like to extend my gratitude to Mr. Vikram Shekhar for editing this book further and Ms, Sindhu Subramanya for the illustrations.

My deepest gratitude goes to my beloved husband Vasudeva G. for being a pillar of strength at each and every step of mine. His constant encouragement has helped me realize my potential. Without him, many things in life would not have been possible. He has made me believe in myself by mirroring my dreams. I thank my children SreeSneha and Mahanth for their co-operation and loyalty. I am ever thankful to my parents for their support and blessings. It would be unfair to forget the support given by my siblings Mamatha and Shivakumar. My cousins Mr. Raju and Mr. Babu have indeed been of great help in the initial stages of my career and I am grateful to the Universe for them.

I cherish the encouragement and love bestowed on me by all my friends and well wishers.

I am thankful to the management to BGS Gleaneagles Global Hospital for timely encouragement and support.

I would also like to thank Mr Pranesh, Prism Books Pvt Ltd for guiding me all the way and being generous enough in publishing this book.

I express my deep sense of gratitude to all those who have guided me in the various stages of my life, especially my teachers.

Contents

Mind Matters

Importance Of Mental Health

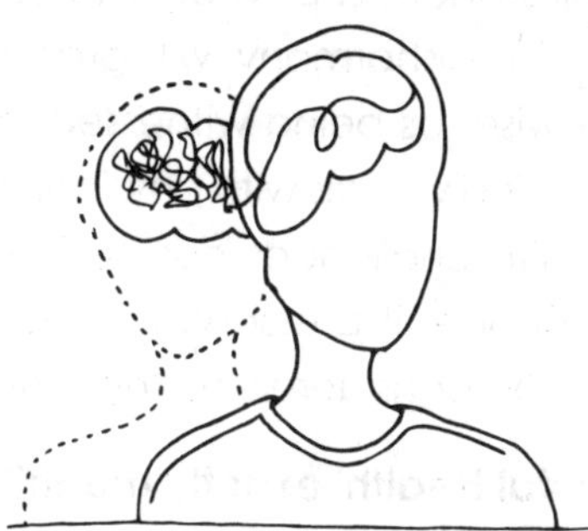

Mental wellbeing is an important aspect of overall health and is often overlooked, while envisioning the bigger picture of 'Health' in general. A positive 'State of Mind' is an 'empowerment' for overall health and good quality of life for an individual, a group and society at large. Despite radical cultural changes and rampant technological advancements, the stigma associated with mental health issues is still looming large, discouraging the masses from seeking much needed help. Mental health has to be taken care of with the same concern, care, attention and enthusiasm as we do for the aspects of physical health. Just like a basic routine and regimen for the body, basic mental healthcare schedule too will keep the Mind and Body (Bodymind) strong and healthy.

1. **We often relate being healthy to only the 'presence' or 'absence' of physical illness (known through symptoms). Where do matters of the mind or mental Health stand when 'Health' in general is conceptualized?**

Health is not just the absence of physical illness. It is a common notion to correlate wellness or wellbeing to physical health. But it is really important to understand the interdependent dimensions of Health. The five main dimensions of Health include 'Physical', 'Mental', 'Intellectual', 'Social' and 'Spiritual'. Each dimension contributes to the other and is inter-connected. A balance or harmony of all these components makes a move towards health of an individual. Disregarding a particular dimension for a lengthy period of time or focusing only on one of them, adversely affects overall health. For instance, a physically healthy individual with emotional and social disharmony will gradually end up with physical illness. Likewise, as being witnessed, during the present Covid-19 pandemic, individuals with physical illness experienced a lot of mental health challenges due to isolation and lack of social interaction. Hence, it is essential to nurture each one of these dimensions to be considered as "healthy".

2. What does 'Mental Health' exactly mean?

Mental health is the state of mind that affects the way a person thinks, feels and behaves. It might be both positive and negative. A positive mental health status enables clarity in feeling and thinking ensuring productivity, whereas poor mental health affects the person's ability to function over a period of time.

3. How much of an influence does the Mind have on the Body? Do issues of the Mind impact at a physical level?

Generally, people consider 'Mind" and 'Body' as separate entities. But in reality, both are intertwined and interconnected, where one is fed by the other. Attention is given more to physical illness because mental illness is not as concrete and tangible as physical illness and it is often overlooked. Mental illness can give a miserable feeling and can hamper day-to-day activities. Most of the times, when attention is not paid to mental states, it manifests as physical issues like vague body pain, pain in the joint, headaches chronic fatigue, etc. There is also a belief that ignoring the symptoms of mental illness will make them disappear. This is rarely true. Keeping mental health issues to oneself may disrupt a normal or healthy life. The bottom-line is: 'We become what we think'.

4. All of us are constantly thinking, worrying and brooding over many things. Does it mean are we all mentally unhealthy? What are the factors that increase the risk of mental illness in a person?

There are multiple factors for mental illness and the onset is gradual. Most common factors that cause mental illness are:

- Genetic factors
- Environment – Poverty and abusive family members, neighbours or colleagues.
- Unhealthy habits (eating and sleeping immediately)
- Stressful events – losing loved ones, loss in business etc.
- Childhood trauma
- Social withdrawal

Most often, environmental factors trigger the illness in a person genetically vulnerable to mental illness.

5. Mental health is very important for our overall well-being. Yet it's not considered important. Why is it so?

Unfortunately, negative attitudes and belief structures towards persons who have mental illness is quite common. Mental health concerns are slowly increasing as it is being viewed with a sense of judgement and also due to the stigma attached to it. This also hinders mentally ill persons from seeking professional help at the right time.

Challenges in seeking help include:

- Stigma regarding mental illness
- Ego issues
- Social concerns regarding other person's opinion, status etc
- Inaccessibility to healthcare
- Unavailability of mental health professionals

6. It is a difficult task to control our Mind. How do we take care of our mental well-being?

Constantly looking after and taking care of our 'State of Mind' is just as important as taking care of our physical body.

Basic Skills To Maintain Mental Well Being

- **Self-compassion:** Doing things to feel good is very sensible. Avoid intense self-criticism (self-condemnation) like "I am not good enough; I am a failure" etc. Such statements are more than likely to affect confidence.

- **Being Expressive:** Hiding and holding-up feelings can cause tensions that affect mental health.

- **Time-management:** Prioritise job work and chores and avoid wasting time on things that cannot be controlled.

- **Social Life:** People with good social connections and networks are generally healthier than those who lack a social web. Spend time with friends and family. In many cases, a person simply needs to feel loved and needed.

- **Healthy Diet:** Food fuels both Mind and Body. Healthy food habits improve mental health.

- **Being Physically Active:** Being active does not mean taking an expensive gym membership and flaunting it. Just walking in a nearby park, cycling etc. are simple yet effective exercises. Any amount of physical activity whether little or large is always better than being idle and sedentary.

❑

Stress

Threshold Crossed

Stress is a normal response and plays its role in many situations in life. Anything within the permitted limits is beneficial and crossing the threshold is utterly damaging. Today's extremely competitive world has inbuilt stress in all the stages of life, right from a childhood to old age. There are innumerable factors to increase stress. Crossing the threshold of stress is just a matter of time, if it is not handled in the right manner. Stress management is an essential skill in present times, so that we are not pushed over the edge.

7. Stress is a commonly used word now. What indeed is Stress? Does being 'stressed out' indicate incapability of handling any situation?

Stress is a normal human response that is experienced by everybody. It is the body's reaction to pressure due to a certain situation or event. The stress response can be physical, mental or emotional. Events triggering stress can range from mundane issues in day-to-day responsibilities like work and family to grave situations such as a new diagnosis, death of a loved one, job change, relationship issues etc.

Stress has three different components. The event that starts a chain of stressful reactions is called 'stressor'. The physical and emotional experiences that follow are 'stress experience' and the behaviour resulting from these experiences is 'stress response'. If stress persists and the person fails to cope, it leads to development of maladjusted stress response

8. In present times, stress is a part and parcel of life. How much of stress should an individual handle?

The stress response and threshold differ from person to person. The first and foremost step is to recognize the stress and its impact on the daily functioning. If a particular period of stress prolongs without relief or relaxation, it can have a bearing on physical health. At times, intensely stressful situations of shorter durations as in completion of a project or a task can only persist till completion which might not be so worrisome. Avoiding stress completely may not be possible, but it always can be managed within the threshold to prevent it affecting day-to-day life. Stress is beneficial in performing better, only if it is for a shorter duration. Persistent stress of long duration indicates that help is urgently needed. Keen observation and alertness about the impact of stress can assist in managing stress effectively.

9. We all are not stressed always. But at certain times, we feel exhausted/overwhelmed by stress. What triggers it?

Common triggers for stress include:

- Changes in sleeping habits
- Change in living conditions
- Beginning of work or loss of job
- Illness
- Relationship issues like marriage, divorce or break-up
- Death of a loved one
- Huge debts
- Adjustment issues, especially to new changes

10. How can we recognize that stress is tiring us out?

Symptoms of chronic stress include:

- Anxiety
- Mood swings
- Irritability
- Headache
- Depression
- Insomnia

11. Just as we keep our weight in check, our stress levels can also be kept in check. What measures can we take to handle the stress levels so that it does not go out of control?

Measures To Be Taken For Management Of Stress

- **Exercise:** Working out regularly is one of the best ways to relax and improve mood. Regularity is of utmost importance.

- **Slowing Down:** Today's fast paced life is extremely hectic and totally demanding. Activities can be done leisurely by taking out adequate time, thus aiding relaxation.

- **Hobbies:** Cultivating hobbies like listening to good music, watching enriching shows on television, reading books, viewing art work etc. can be stress relieving.

- **Nature Time:** Spending time in calm, serene places can help a lot.

- **Meditation:** Practices like meditation helps to quieten the Mind.

- **Quality Time:** Try to do something every day which boosts energy levels. It does not have to be a long duration activity. Even a short duration (15-30 minutes) activity will suffice.

❑

The Nervous Breakdown

Anxiety

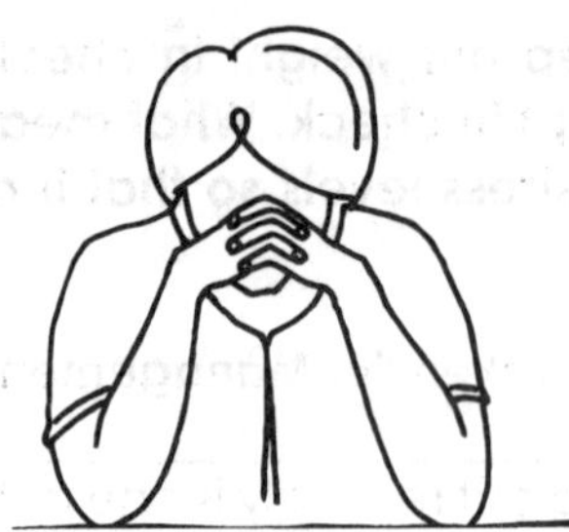

Sometimes The magnitude of problems arising from anxiety is most often underestimated. Anxiety is commonly perceived as a simple issue. But on the contrary, it can have farfetched impact on the individual. Uncontrolled anxiety turning into panic attacks can give a sense of impending doom presenting as emergencies to the hospital, only to be ruled out as an anxiety disorder. Preventing such breakdowns and panic attacks calls for tackling anxiety, at the initial stage itself.

12. Commonly, everybody relates anxiety to fear and stress. What exactly does anxiety mean?

Anxiety is the body's response to stress and new situations like first day of the job, public speaking, attending an interview or taking a test. It is normal to feel anxious in such situations. This is a transient feeling and does not interfere with the routine.

13. Few people get anxious for every single thing and few others handle it well. Why that difference?

Each and every challenge is an opportunity for growth and improvement. Each one of us is striving to become a better person in life and beyond. In the process, some choose to embrace the challenge and joyfully learn from their experience and few others choose to rebel against it. Individuals who are perfectionists or who are timid or those who intend to control and direct everything as per their wishes, develop anxiety. It is a matter of perspective. Our perception of the world is what creates our life experiences. A particular perspective leads to a particular interpretation of the experience. This might lead to anxiety. All problems in life have two main possibilities:

- Striving to overcome the problem and achieving the outcome.
- Justifying and accepting that it is impossible to overcome the problem.

It all depends on what is opted for. Instead of getting trapped with questions like "Oh why me?" asking "Oh why not?" shifts the focus. Persons who ask 'why not' questions to themselves are less prone to anxiety. Questioning the thought patterns brings a conscious awareness about the situation which makes it easier to stay in control. It is important to bear in mind that worrying about getting rid of anxiety, makes it even worse than it is. In short, persons with good lifestyles and positive outlooks handle anxiety better.

14. Whenever we face challenging situations, we normally feel anxious about it. What is the normal way of handling anxiety at that time?

 **Measures To Be Taken For Management Of Stress**

- **Breathing exercises:** Take a deep breath and slowly breathe out. This is to be repeated until we feel calm. Focussing on breathing will lower down the heart rate and the thought rush thus helping in spreading a feeling of calm and serenity. Try to name the sensations and feelings. This keeps uncomfortable feelings at bay and brings in clarity. This is a powerful technique because we cannot breathe deeply and be anxious at the same time.

- **Divert attention:** The moment anxiety symptoms start manifesting and disturbing us, divert attention thus: chat with friends, watch favourite shows, paint or do an engrossing chore. This, shifts focus.

- **Immediate physical activity:** Brisk walking or alteration of positions like sitting to standing, stretching or getting up from the bed and washing the face etc. helps in changing the sensory stimulus and thus the sensory experience. It is an excellent way to use up excess energy.

- **Hydration:** Drinking sufficient water helps to reduce anxiety symptoms. Hydration status can influence the mood.

- **Feeling safe:** Anxiety causes restlessness and drives imagination towards negativity and uncertainty. Awareness in the present moment and self-questioning like "What is there to fear about?" and "Am I safe?" helps in staying grounded and feeling less anxious.

15. Examinations, major events that involve interaction with persons such as gatherings, sports events, stage events, interviews, meetings etc. induce performance anxiety. What is the technique of dealing with this and performing to the best of one's ability?

Public speaking, stage performance, attending an interview and examination, induces a feeling of nervousness. This in-turn increases the heart rate, pulse rate and causes sweaty palms. It is normal. Anxiety is not always harmful. It in fact, aids in better performance due to fear of failure. But anxiety should not hinder the performance by simply anticipating a stressful event.

 **TIPS TO OVERCOME PERFORMANCE ANXIETY**

- Practice well and be prepared.

- Avoid self-doubting thoughts and persons who discourage and de-motivate.

- Stay away from "what if?" questions.

- Take a deep breath and relax.
- Stop comparing and judging yourself.
- Be in the present.
- Feel confident and stay optimistic.
- Don't skip food. Drink water and keep yourself hydrated.
- Visualize positive outcome.
- Be open to new learning.

16. In times of severe anxiety, it becomes very difficult to control it. The more we want to stop anxiety, the more it goes out of hand and we feel extremely uncomfortable. Is it normal or does this indicates that professional intervention is needed?

Certainly, help from a mental health professional is needed to overcome anxiety with the above-mentioned symptoms.

Here are a few signs that indicate one needs help:

- Inability to control thought rush
- Sleep disturbance due to restlessness
- Negative self-talk
- Social withdrawal
- Panic attacks and sensing impending danger and doom
- Breathlessness and palpitation.
- Trouble concentrating and inability to perform well personally and professionally
- Fatigue
- Tremors
- Overwhelming fear

These symptoms may not go away on their own and may get even worse if not treated. Please do seek professional help immediately. Early intervention definitely helps.

17. How to detect whether anxiety is leading to a panic attack?

Signs of panic attack include the following:

- A panic attack causes sudden unreasonable fear with strong physical symptoms for unreal situations, whereas anxiety attacks increase gradually and is often associated with triggers.
- Panic attacks tend to peak and usually come down within few minutes; whereas anxiety symptoms will persist for a longer duration. At times, it may be difficult to distinguish between anxiety and panic attack because they have similar physical and emotional symptoms.
- It is possible to go through the daily routine with anxiety symptoms whereas panic attacks are severe and hamper the daily routine.
- Physical symptoms are severe in panic attacks when compared to anxiety.

18. It is best that we do not let anxiety go into a panic mode. What can be done to prevent panic attacks?

Anxiety is the most common mental health condition. Recognising the symptoms and triggers of anxiety empowers the individual to inculcate changes in order to prevent panic attacks. Here are a few changes that can be practiced:

MEASURES TO PREVENT PANIC ATTACK

- **Being physically active:** Regular exercise and yoga breaks the anxious thought pattern and diverts the attention from mind to the body.
- **Questioning thoughts:** Introspecting about reality and relevance of thoughts is a good exercise which in turn can help reassure oneself.
- **Balanced diet:** Consume a well-balanced diet with optimum hydration and avoid junk food. It is also important to note whether anxiety worsens after eating.

- **Adequate sleep:** Sleeping at the same time each night is a good practice. Avoid binge watching and using phone prior to sleep.
- **Meditation:** Meditation gradually helps to spend most of the time in the present moment. It improves the ability to mindfully manage anxiety. It is crucial to meditate under supervision.
- **Interaction with peer group:** Talking to individuals with similar issues, sharing experiences with friends and family gives them the opportunity to render help in much better ways. Talk to a psychologist for professional help.

❑

Depression

The Red Alert

Battling depression is indeed a "red alert" as an increasing number of suicide cases, due to underlying depression are on the rise. With good support system and professional help at the right time, individuals can come out of depression successfully and stay out of it.

19. Depression has been in the lime light for the past few years. Why is depression increasing gradually?

Addressing any problem or issue in the initial stage itself prevents it from growing into something large. Depression is one such issue which blows out of proportion if not addressed initially. Changes in life-style are contributing to the vulnerability for depression. The fast-paced life (referred to as life in the fast lane) is hampering the quality of life, as it gives more scope for intense competition and comparison. The bygone generations to a large extent were relatively happier and content with what was available to them. This was seen in their meaningful family outings with close relatives, personal face-to-face interactions with others and not being pressurized to own consumer durables and latest gizmos. On the contrary, the whole scenario of life has changed now. Increased use of smart phones/gizmos and virtual interactions on various social media platforms has radically altered the nature of social interactions. The influence of Internet has brought about a cultural shift, which has created a false sense of independence and a dearth of socializing. Easy and quick accessibility to information with the flick of fingers, stressful jobs, prolonged working hours, uncertainty in continuation of jobs, unreasonable targets and overall unhealthy lifestyle is all piling up together and providing more scope for depression to set in and become chronic. The constant yearning to earn more money with less and less effort, focussing more on the pleasures of party culture and weekend trips, have made an individual forget the beauty of small joys. Hence, most of them are constantly complaining and are dissatisfied. Unfortunately, a healthy behaviour has become alien to today's life. Despite all these drastic changes in life and society, persons with mental health problems still experience discrimination and stigma. This prevents many from opening up about their depression. Issues come to light only after adverse and untoward events take place.

20. The current life style is hectic and stressful for almost everybody. What are the other factors that increase the risk of causing depression?

Similar to stress and anxiety, each person's response to life situations and circumstances varies vastly. For a given situation, as in a family facing a long-term stressful situation like the death of a family member, some get depressed and others do not. This is because of differences in personality and the respective response to the handling of grief. The support system around us influences the outcome too. People who socialize are less likely to get depressed. At the same time, social conditioning which determines a set response for certain life events and situations also do not let individuals express their response completely. This in turn leads to suppression and depression in the long run.

It is difficult to point out the exact cause and is generally multi-factorial. Common causes include:

- Death of loved ones
- Abuse (physical and mental)
- Divorce or separation
- Serious illness
- Hereditary causes
- Unemployment/poverty
- Retirement

It all depends on what is opted for. Instead of getting trapped with questions like "Oh why me?" asking "Oh why not?" shifts the focus. Persons who ask 'why not' questions to themselves are less prone to anxiety. Questioning the thought patterns brings a conscious awareness about the situation which makes it easier to stay in control. It is important to bear in mind that worrying about getting rid of anxiety, makes it even worse than it is. In short, persons with good lifestyles and positive outlooks handle anxiety better.

21. Many individuals might be battling depression and most of them would not even realize that they are depressed to the extent that requires help. What are the early signs of depression?

Signs and symptoms of depression differ from person to person. The signs can be temporary as a part of life's normal lows. But its persistence and ill effects on the quality of life especially on thoughts, feelings and behaviour demands attention.

A few early signs of depression are:

- **Lack of interest:** A person with depression tends to withdraw from activities that were once enjoyable and satisfying.
- **Mood swings:** Intolerant to others, feeling irritable, anxious and hopeless. Crying for no reason or feeling tearful.
- **Lack of socialization:** Avoiding meeting or talking to friends and relatives.

- **Lack of self-care:** Neglecting cleanliness and hygiene.
- **Lack of concentration:** Avoiding going to work and finding it difficult to work due to lack of concentration.
- **Changes in sleep pattern:** Either excess sleepiness (Somnambulism) or sleeplessness (Insomnia).
- **Changes in appetite:** Eating less or more depending on the symptoms which results in weight loss or gain.
- **Vague physical symptoms:** Complaints of aches and pains.
- **Suicidal thoughts:** Suicidal tendencies need immediate attention and treatment.

22. Once a diagnosis of depression is made. What next?

Dealing with the diagnosis of depression is very crucial.

- Firstly, get treated by a psychiatrist and adhere to the medicine prescribed.
- Consult a psychologist to learn new ways to cope and manage depression.
- Modify life style as a healthy lifestyle helps to reduce the impact of depression.
- Educate oneself about depression and the ways and means to cope with it.
- Try staying active and occupied by spending time with friends and family.

❑

Self-Doubt

The Alarm

Self-doubt is the constant alarm ringing within, which prompts one to cross-check everything said and done, with a sense of doubtfulness. It is nurtured within from a long time with unknowing assistance from parents, persons around and circumstances. Self-doubt lowers self-esteem and inhibits the individuals from realizing their full potential. It is never too late to come out of this shell and shutting down the alarm, rather than snoozing it.

23. It is always good to check oneself before speaking or acting to be more thoughtful and careful. Is this self -doubt?

Self-doubt is doubting one's own abilities by degrading and devaluing one-self. These self-limiting negative thoughts put one down in comparison with others. Hence, the full potential is not achieved and also there is low confidence to try out something new. If not amended at the right time, it grows along with the person. It is important for parents and teachers to provide support to the individual to help overcome the feeling by appreciating their effort rather than success. Being mindful of thoughts and actions is important. But persistent self-degradation indicates self-doubt.

24. Right from our school days to our working days, so many of us have experienced that, despite knowing the right things and having brilliant ideas, we hesitate in expressing it. We have low self confidence. What are the other signs to recognise that we have self-doubt?

Low confidence is one aspect of self-doubt. Self-doubt can be recognised by the following signs:

- **Fear of failure:** Avoiding responsibility in attempting new ideas and challenges due to constant self-doubt and relying on others help and decisions.
- **Negative thoughts:** Negative self-talk and devaluing own strength by imagining bad outcomes and consequences which gradually lower and degrade self-confidence.
- **Social withdrawal:** Withdrawal from friends and family due to fear of peer rejection. Inability to express opinion and speak-up despite being unhappy with others decisions.
- **Comparison with peers:** Every individual is unique and special. Comparison with others will always make oneself to be weighed down. It is like expecting monkeys to swim and fish to climb trees. Focussing more on strengths will give confidence.
- **Company of toxic individuals:** Spending time with persons who constantly give negative feedback, who label and judge everything, will tend to make us question ourselves by doubting our strengths. It is best to stay far away from such toxic persons.

25. Self-doubt gets inculcated at a very young age and is carried forward. What influences this trait at a young age?

Home is the child's first school and parents have the maximum influence on the child, especially in the first decade of life. Parenting mistakes can impact child's confidence and give rise to self-doubt.

All parents expect their children to excel in whatever they do. It is an unrealistic expectation that children have to be perfect in all activities. Each one of us tends to commit the same mistakes which our parents did. In this bargain and tug-of-war between right and wrong, we end up blaming and labelling children by sowing the seed of self-doubt.

A few common errors committed by parents:

- **Too many instructions**: It is important to allow children to explore, learn and do things independently. When they follow the instructions, they do not feel a sense of accomplishment, as they feel that they were supported through and through. This indirectly makes them more and more dependent.

- **Fault finding**: As a parent, it is easy to find fault in children. Constant blaming and correcting them makes them feel low. Instead shift the focus from outcome to their effort. This helps them improve.

- **Name calling/labelling**: Name calling is usually done during some activity or play time. When children are called *stupid, bossy, selfish, liar, lazy etc*. they tend to receive and start seeing themselves the same way. This forms strong impressions in their mind.

- **Being over protective**: Mistakes teach children the do's and don'ts and encourages them to think creatively. Imposing ideas, creating favourable atmosphere and protecting them always will not help in any way at all. Permitting children to learn by the trial-and-error method will teach them to fix the problem by themselves.

- **Comfort zone:** Permitting children to try out new things will bring them out of the comfort zone and make them bold and decisive. Adapting to new changes is hard and fear of negative consequences always predominates in the mind of the child. But once they start, they realize it is not as they presumed it to be. It is vital to teach children to face life as it is head on.

26. Confidence is the key in many situations and can be a win-win strategy. Self-doubt can drag us down to failure. What are the other pitfalls of having self-doubt?

Constant self-doubt can lead to:

- Low self-esteem
- Anxiety
- Depression
- Lack of motivation
- Difficulty in decision making

27. How to overcome self-doubt and develop the right level of confidence?

SUGGESTIONS TO OVERCOME SELF-DOUBT

- **Stop comparing:** The idea of success is different to different persons. It is inappropriate to compare our weakness with others strength. Comparison with our previous performance helps in improvement.

- **Stop over-thinking:** Negative self-talk will drain energy and increase stress. Bringing thoughts to the present moment and not following the negative thoughts will break the process of over-thinking.

- **Understand the triggers:** Avoid fuelling negative past experiences which evoke uncomfortable feelings. Knowing a root cause of any problem itself is a big win. Learn to challenge the challenge.

- **Being kind to ourselves:** Reflect on all thoughts and actions at the end of the day. Celebrate and appreciate small changes. Shift the focus from negative to positive. Accept both strengths and weaknesses.

- **Seek professional help:** Sharing our feelings with people who support us unconditionally makes a huge difference. Sometimes all we want is a good listener so that we can unburden. If the problem persists, seek thorough professional help from a psychologist. Psychotherapy is one potential method of treating self-doubt.

❑

Failure

The Stepping Stone

Failure always has a negative shade to it. It is the perception that gives it the negative tinge. A glass can be viewed as half full or half empty. Similarly, failure should not be viewed as being unsuccessful and instead should be viewed as a stepping stone to success. Failure brings new lessons along with it which puts us on the right path to success.

28. All of us begin endeavours with a wish of being successful as nobody wants to fail. Failure considered is an insult. Is failure a sign of inefficiency?

Failure is an inability to perform as expected. It is always viewed negatively and as contradictory to success. We forget to acknowledge that we learn from them. The lessons from failure are more enduring than lessons from victories. Playing safe is riskier than we think. Playing safe seems easier as failure and embarrassment can be avoided. Failure makes us stronger and eventually increases confidence. We should not let failure define us. Constant effort to try and try enables learning. Introspecting on reasons for failure and willingness to learn from it will help take necessary corrective actions in the subsequent attempts and ultimately aid growth. This helps in building resilience

29. Expecting success is a positive frame of mind. Yet we fail sometimes. Why so?

Reasons for failure range from deliberate deviation to thoughtful experimentation.

- **Lack of self-belief/low self esteem :** Life gives both positive and negative experiences. But unfortunately, negative is the one which has a long lasting impression and gives a low feeling. Initially, avoiding challenges might seem safe. But it often skips our notice that, at the same time, simultaneously doubt and fear are reinforced in greater strength. Low self-esteem will thus be a barrier in facing new challenges at all times and will also increase social withdrawal.
- **Comparison :** Many a times, we don't even try due to a fear of being judged by others. Everyone is unique and special in their own ways. But we often compare others best work, their performance and features against our average ones. Instead, self-motivation to compete with ourselves and our earlier performances is worth the while. The only way out of this is "being our natural self". When the energy and focus shifts to ourselves, there is a huge scope for improvement and success.
- **Unclear goals :** Lack of clarity about the goal will divert our energy and time to the wrong place. Lack of goal in turn leads to lack of target or focus and this will set in a flow of life that is out of gear and ultimately out of control. It is hard to swim against the flow. Clear goal setting will direct the focus on the right target and this smooth flow will ensure success.
- **Defensive to feedbacks:** Opportunities for self-improvement are limited by being defensive about positive criticism, suggestions, ideas and opinions from others. Open mindedness to receive feedback is essential and attention should be paid to the feedback and not to our response to it. It is important to understand others' perspective with clarity and also appreciate their concerns. Each circumstance is

different. Assess the value of feedback and decide how and when to follow it.

- **Lack of practice and commitment:** Many fail even with the best of resources. The main reason for this is lack of practice. Practice is very essential to achieve or to perform as expected. Attention and repetition help to acquire new skills and knowledge. As the wise said: Practice makes Man perfect.

30. Failure is always considered as shameful. Failing in anything small or big is a mighty blow. How to deal with it?

 **SUGGESTIONS TO COPE WITH FAILURE**

- **Keep calm and accept the reality:** Always admit mistakes and take steps and measures to rectify them. It is always easy to find solutions when the ocean of the mind is calm and composed. Take responsibility for all actions and work on it. Never stop trying.

- **Be optimistic:** An optimistic mindset will affect our choices and actions. Being optimistic in stressful situations helps in better decision making and comprehending totally that failure is temporary.

- **Take responsibility for consequences:** Taking responsibility for failure is indeed difficult. Persons who take responsibility are more resilient compared to those who end up blaming others and external factors. Taking responsibility helps a lot in moving forward and making progress.

- **Self-introspection:** Failure is an unpleasant feeling. Only a handful of them take failure as an opportunity to learn from mistakes and improve or work on it. Always introspecting on reasons for failure measures to fix it and changes to be undertaken, gives invaluable inner strength.

- **Come out of comfort zone:** Walking out of the comfort zone is the most difficult thing to do. But it brings a significant difference in the confidence level. ☞

- **Never stop trying:** Albert Einstein once said, "You never fail until you stop trying". We cannot expect a 'success story' in our life without even trying. Every attempt is a flight towards excellence. Patience and perseverance are the keys.

❑

The Appeal

Body Image

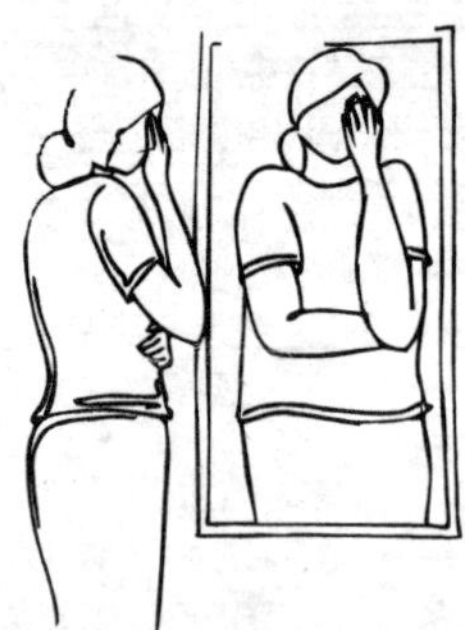

Appearances do create the first impression when we interact with others and the first impression is considered to be the best impression. Importance to physical appearance has been there for a long time in human society. But there have been new additions to the appeal factor due to the mass media revolution. It is not just about how to look good; it is about how to look appealing in the very first instance. In the intricate maze of appeal and applause, we have lost track of the sacred path to inner beauty.

31. Appearance plays a very important role as it gives the first impression of us to those with whom we interact with. What is the body image that gives the best impression?

The concept of a "perfect" body does not really exist. So, chasing the perfect body can end only in total disappointment. There is no set standard for the best body image or appearance. Body image is influenced by both external and internal factors. External factors include social factors such as culture, media and interactions with family and friends. Internal factors include mental and emotional status of the individual. Body image is the mental picture that we have of ourselves and the way we feel about it. These form a collective representation of our strengths and weaknesses as we see them. The body image can be positive or negative.

32. No two individuals are the same. Each one looks different. Yet, most of us are unsatisfied with some of our features like height, weight, complexion etc. In addition to it, others also comment on the same. Is this body shaming?

Body shaming is the act of criticism or mocking a person's physical size, shape and appearance. This act of humiliating someone is not just limited to fat or thin. It comprises comments on others dressing, looks, physical features and certain attributes like hair colour, scars, wearing spectacles etc.

33. Body shaming is degrading of the self or others which hurts and leaves behind deep impression. What makes some persons behave in this manner?

Body shaming others indicates lack of acceptance of self and a tendency to project it on to others due to feelings of extreme insecurity deep inside. When acceptance is positive, good in others will inspire and when acceptance is negative it leads to jealousy. The main reason behind the insensitive comments is lack of compassion and empathy. Added to this, in the present times, social media platforms and television shows also influence this behaviour. Mocking and bullying on screen in the name of humour has also increased. It is seriously, a conflicting messaging to society. Body shaming is bad when kids do it in school, but highly profitable when adults do it in front of camera!

34. What is the impact of body shaming?

Body shaming plays one of the major roles in destroying a child's personality and mental health. No one is born perfect, yet many of us have been bullied at some point in our life and it happens with many children. When a child is body shamed, we often take it lightly. But it can land a heavy blow on confidence levels and can lead to low self esteem and a lack of confidence. Body shaming can have a severe impact on mental health.

Body shaming is humiliating with often painful and long-term consequences. The effect of this will be carried into adulthood. Adults with negative image may feel ashamed or be too self-conscious due to comparison.

Research also indicates that higher body dissatisfaction is associated with poorer quality of life as there is a higher risk of developing mood disorders, eating disorders, lower self-esteem, relationship issues, social anxiety and depression.

35. Body image issues generally begin in teenage years. With increased social media influence now, even younger children have body image issues. How to recognise this?

Now, teenagers have a very clear perception on what the perfect body is supposed to look like. For girls, perfect body is a flat tummy, no acne and good height. For boys, it is a toned muscular body with perfect teeth, no acne and good height. Persistent obsession with this is unhealthy. The earlier these problems are identified, the easier they are to fix. Few indications of body image issues in children include:

- Constant comparison with friends and relatives could mean that something much more serious is fuelling those thoughts.
- Changes in eating habits like refusing to eat their favourite snacks and eating less during meal time.
- Dissatisfaction about clothes worn not looking good on them and trying countless outfits.
- Avoiding social gatherings.
- Mood swings and anger outbursts.

36. How to reconcile with this? How to overcome this insecurity regarding body image?

The concept of body and body image has to be dealt with in childhood itself so that at no point in life, feelings of insecurity in this matter emerge. Counselling children is important to instil confidence in them. Along with what is taught, children also imbibe parents' attitude and behaviour by mere observation. Attention should be paid to both these aspects.

SUGGESTIONS TO DEAL WITH BODY IMAGE ISSUES

- **Convey positive messages to children:** Exposure to messages in the media or society regarding appearance, parents' attitude about looks (height, weight etc.) is passed on unintentionally. It is extremely important to ensure that we are not contributing to negative messages. For instance, talking about weight loss and dieting makes children absorb the message that weight loss is a worthy goal. Avoid talking about dieting in front of children.

- **Stop mocking others:** Mocking others appearance makes children feel that it is OK! to do so. Instead turn these moments into teachable ones.

- **Reiterate healthy food habits:** Practice and teach healthy food habits as a routine. Avoid projecting exercise as a punishment for over eating. This sets children up to hook physical exercises with being fat.

- **Develop compassion:** Compassion towards self and others makes one accept others as they are. Practising self-love is important. Acceptance of our flaws, in fact empowers us to shield and fight our own battles. Acceptance gives emotional tranquillity. Non acceptance gives rise to negative emotions. When hurt is not accepted, it creates hatred. When it is accepted, forgiveness and unconditional love blossoms.

- **Empathetic listening:** One of the best things to do is to listen with empathy rather than jumping to conclusions to fix the problem immediately.

- **Appreciating qualities:** Appreciate each person's individuality and uniqueness. Avoid comparing children with friends and relatives. Reinforce that their 'value' lies in their qualities and not in their appearance or body image. Compliment children for their strength, skills and values in life.

37. In today's world, having a social media image is more important and this is often driven by ones' looks. We often tend to copy others in their looks and dressing to garner attention. Beauty has been redefined. What is the right message about beauty and body in this context?

Today's society has set certain standards of beauty that are followed by a large number of persons. These standards are also responsible for creating personality complex among those who fail to meet this standard. As a result, many often base their lives on the wrong notion of beauty. Consequently, adolescents of the current generation have more challenges while dealing with body image issues. These issues begin even earlier than the teenage years with many young children also expressing unhappiness about their body.

A lot of the negative body image comes from internal views of oneself. Shifting conversations from how one looks to how one feels will redirect children's thoughts about their choices.

Teaching children the importance of inner beauty is vital because that is what enhances external beauty. It is the strength of relationships too. Finally inner beauty cannot be judged and it is that which gives one the confidence to face the world head on.

It is very important for an individual to feel confident, comfortable and happy about their body as thinking influences feelings. A positive body image can boost our physical, mental, social, emotional and spiritual wellbeing.

❑

Social Media

The Instant Connect

Social media is the fastest way to connect with anybody in any nook or corner of the world instantly and that too without even moving an inch. It also brings goodies like engaging wider audiences in shorter period of time span, controlling how we present ourselves to others and choosing to showcase only certain aspects of our life. Faster connections, big circle of friends, presence in multiple groups all virtually make up a 'virtual world'. This instant connect in the virtual world is distancing humans from the real world.

38. Social media presence is considered a necessity today. Moreover, the pandemic situation has set in a new normal of attending schools, colleges and work from home which has reinforced virtual interactions. Is this boon or bane from mental health perspective?

The concept of a "perfect" body does not really exist. So, chasing the perfect body can end only in total disappointment. There is no set standard for the best body image or appearance. Body image is influenced by both external and internal factors.

External factors include social factors such as culture, media and interactions with family and friends. Internal factors include mental and emotional status of the individual. Body image is the mental picture that we have of ourselves and the way we feel about it. These form a collective representation of our strengths and weaknesses as we see them. The body image can be positive or negative.

39. Social media interactions have increased as it is easier and faster to communicate and exchange ideas. Social media time takes away a huge chunk of our time every day. Is this harmful?

Definitely yes, it is harmful. Humans are social beings. Being socially connected to friends and family add years to life and life to years. Social media itself is not a problem. It is the way it is utilized which has made way for addictive behaviour like constantly watching updates and notifications. Sometimes, people are so lost in the virtual world on the phone that they don't even know who sits next to them while using public transport. Every single thing seems possible with the phone like paying bills online, shopping online, online bank transactions etc. which gives such a sense of independence and need for less socialization. Spending a lot of time on social media and being hooked to the screen also results in lack of physical activity leading to obesity. Light from phone screens disrupts the sleep cycle by keeping one awake for longer hours and this eventually results in insomnia. Finally, spending a lot of time in the virtual world can have a negative impact on many more aspects such as the following:

- **Lower self-esteem:** Priority to virtual self-image than the real one.
- **Loss of cognitive ability:** Poor concentration and weak memory
- **Strains to the eyes and body:** Spending long hours on phone strains the eyes and also affects the body postures and can cause stiffness and pain in both neck and shoulders.

40. Adolescents and youth are influenced the most by social media. Why is it so?

Adolescents and youth are obsessed with the idea of their presence in the virtual world. They constantly check their mobile phones now and then. They also give more importance to online appearance and virtual image than the real one. Their hands and thoughts are always busy with smart phones and they fail to focus on their immediate responsibilities. 'Likes' on social media is another trigger for youth to keep checking their mobile phones. They fail to know the psychology of 'likes'. Marketing is the basis of 'likes' on social media. Liked posts and its related content keep popping up often and often. It is sheer business. Not realizing this, there is a drive to attain more likes just out of comparison and competition which can damage mental health. This highlights the lack of value-based education. Another common characteristic of youth is to create a likable virtual view of their life and most of their time is spent in getting photos clicked. They fail to enjoy the present moment. More importance is given to looks and likes. If they find their friends updating their 'status' with new photos and images, with new looks, the pressure on the others just explodes. They strive hard to match and post photos. This triggers body image issues which makes them compare and induce feelings of shame and guilt. This leads to unnecessary dieting. If they have had a bad day, going on social media and seeing friends having a great time can make it even worse. They tend to compare themselves to only the best part of someone else's life. This results in anger, jealousy, frustration and loneliness. The social media network is such that it makes the youth think a lot and feel a little.

41. Most often even adults have 'Fear of Missing Out' (FOMO) due to social media posts, though they have the awareness and understanding that social media presence is not real. Why does this happen?

As already mentioned, we humans are social beings. Meeting friends and relatives face-to-face is beneficial for our mental, social and emotional well-being. Social media has made our lives easy by connecting us to the whole world. It is easier to find old pals by just searching online. Sharing, inviting, payments, shopping and so many more facilities are available at our finger tips. But the excessive, unmindful use of this has become so toxic that even adults are driven by looks and are in a competitive mode to showcase that they are also living their life to the fullest. Few reasons of even adults being victims of FOMO are:

- **Comparison:** Most often comparison makes us feel better or worse off than our friends and relatives. Falling into the spiral of comparing and contrasting makes us judgemental and also raises doubts about self-worth.
- **Peer pressure:** Peer pressure drives content on social media and also leads to obsessive monitoring of the phone to keep up with activities of the friends.
- **Failure to understand the reality:** Virtual world makes us forget reality and strengthens the assumption that others' posts are real. We fail to acknowledge that only portrayed best moments of life are shared online and nobody's life is perfect. Hence, we eventually end up trying to match or overdo it.
- **Self-absorption:** Extreme self-centredness and seeking external validation further enhances FOMO in self and others.

42. What are the signs of FOMO?

FOMO can be an issue if most of these signs are present for a considerable period of time. The signs include:

- Excessive use of social media
- Importance to others' opinions and validation
- Lack of physical activity due to social media
- Failure to complete a task on time
- Low life satisfaction due to comparison
- Feeling very low on missing out something on social media
- Seeking a lot of attention by clicking pictures of everything that is done.

- Feeling restless with phone
- Fear of not being around on special occasions
- Tracking likes constantly

43. Options for social media interactions are increasing at a fast pace now with many options like 'status updates' in Whatsapp, Instagram, Facebook, Snapchats etc. How to protect our mental health in this era of virtual reality?

The social media boom is beneficial in many ways as it is easy to connect, learn and share important information. But it can be detrimental to mental health when it is used unhealthily. Here are a few tips to protect your mental health.

TIPS TO PROTECT MENTAL HEALTH FROM HARMFUL USE OF SOCIAL MEDIA

- **Limit social media time:** Try to avoid using mobile to wish close friends on birthdays, anniversaries etc. Wish them directly. Turn off notifications. It is a major distraction and also prompts repeated phone usage. Be cautious about posting or sharing on social media. A self-check on the purpose of sharing or posting anything will aid in posting only relevant and appropriate content.

- **Avoid using social media before bed time:** Using social media before going to bed might alter the sleep time and pattern. Watching anything for a longer time or watching unwanted stuff prolongs the waking time. Always be clear and specific. Avoid binge watching.

- **Being observant of our feelings:** Observing ourselves regarding what we do and how we feel on social media, each time we use it, will guide us on its usage too. Feelings of stress, peer pressure, low satisfaction are indicators of limiting the screen time.

- **Being in the present:** Online connection cannot replace real life interactions. Connecting with people in person enhances social life and acts as a protective shield.

- **Being mindful:** Being mindful when choosing and connecting with friends online is very important. Giving likes to everything we see and accepting all friend requests is not a good sign. Accept a friend request only if it is needed. Following the heart and liking a post genuinely is good as it will not encourage others also to post unnecessary content.

- **Stay physically active and prioritize self-care:** Regular exercise, yoga, meditation keeps us fit both mentally and physically. Importantly, avoid mobile phone use while eating.

- **Engage more in real world activities:** Talking to people around will improve social life. Volunteering towards social causes such as helping animals and people in the community is more worthwhile. Offline activities help in boosting self-esteem and improves mood.

- **Avoid comparison with others:** Comparison with others keeps us dwelling in negative thought patterns. Instead, it is good to focus on our strengths. It lessens the impact of FOMO and improves overall mental well-being.

- **Remember- we are in-charge:** Keeping a regular check on social media timing and content is extremely important. Only we can control what we see and whom we connect to. Actively prioritize what needs to be done and what to disconnect.

- **Don't hesitate to seek help:** Burn outs happen to anyone, anytime and anywhere. Seek timely help when it is hard to cope up and overcome social media addiction. Being kind and helpful to ourselves is the first step.

44. In the last few years, we have heard a lot of incidents of behavioural issues in children, adolescents' and young adults and cases of suicide too due to influence of mobile phones, social media and gaming addiction. How to prevent this?

These issues indicate that it is not addressed or identified by friends and family in the initial stages. Spending time on social media has become common for most parents and they also justify it by saying that they need to stay updated and up to the mark. But remember, children are smart and they see and imitate parents. Children also assume that their parents are always right. So, there is high possibility of mirroring parents' behaviour. It is good to begin by asking two important questions:

A. Is it ok if our children follow the same habits as of the elders in the house?

B. Are we ready to face the consequences?

If your answer is an emphatic "No", then here are few measures to prevent them.

PREVENTIVE MEASURES FOR ADDICTIVE BEHAVIOUR IN CHILDREN AND ADOLESCENTS

- **Model good behaviour and set an example:** Having healthy habits will definitely nurture the mind and body. If not, it is harder for children to understand the outcome when parents themselves are doing it in plain sight.

- **Educate children:** It is important to have an open conversation about the pros and cons of social media. Educate them on privacy and other related issues. Privacy is not just clicking on "friends" or "public". Sharing email address and personal details on different sites is also harmful and dangerous. Educate them on how photos, videos and comments made online can be misused. Warn children about not sharing their personal details with total strangers. Let them know how fake photos are displayed and cannot be retrieved later as they can disappear anytime.

- **Be vigilant:** Supervise children's social media accounts and appreciate them when they follow instructions. Use applications for parental supervision which monitors and also notifies in cases of inappropriate content. Educate them regarding the finer aspects of online safety.

- **Brief them about the consequences:** Once do's and don'ts are explained, tell the children what will happen if they break rules. Repeat the conversation about social media as often as it feels appropriate because they are often exposed to new platforms.

- **Encourage real life relationships:** Meeting friends and relatives face-to-face is so important in developing the skills needed to understand other people's moods and emotions. It also helps them to learn non-verbal cues and facial gestures of people which help them to develop empathy.
- **Engage them in physical activities:** Encourage children to engage in physical activities like cycling, playing with friends and also to keep their rooms and surroundings clean. Take their help in age-appropriate household chores like cleaning table after meal, setting the shoe stand etc. By doing this, they feel important worthy and also responsible.
- **Seek help:** Don't hesitate to reach out to a mental health professional if you notice these red flag signs:
- Children being always busy online, watching videos, scrolling screen up and down.
  - Avoiding interacting with people in real life by being isolated and lonely.
  - Decrease in physical activity.
  - Poor academic performance.
  - Sleep disturbances.

❑

Peer Pressure

Friend Or Foe?

A friend in need is a friend indeed. Such true friends are truly rare in life. As children we have a big circle of friends and as we grow up, we are left with few friends. We realize the meaning and depth of friendships gradually. It is commonly assumed that only children are more prone to get affected by peer pressure. Quite surprisingly, it does affect adults too. If there is a negative influence by a friend at any stage of life, then that person is more a foe than a friend. At times, it is inevitable to deal with such people. The trick is to know how to handle it in such a way that we are still part of the peer group, but remain unaffected by the pressure.

45. Friends are people with whom we share comfortable spaces and have fun. Having friends is always a pleasure. When does it start to convert into peer pressure?

A friend is someone who makes our life colourful and joyful by making each moment a sweet memory. A good friend accepts us the way we are, supports us through tough times and trusts us. Mainly, there is freedom to express our views with them and our disapprovals are also respected and valued.

Peer pressure starts when there is fear of rejection (trying to match them by wearing similar clothes, walking and talking like them) and a desire to fit in and adapt to the values and practices of the peer group. In short, it starts when we are being forced to do things that make us feel uncomfortable.

A quick introspection in these situations will help us identify that peer pressure is setting in.

- Does meeting friends seem stressful?
- Having issues about image and being too image conscious?
- Is there feeling of insecurity to express views?
- Does it feel necessary to impress friends always?

46. Does peer pressure apply only to children and teenagers?

Absolutely not/No Unfortunately, peer pressure is experienced by all age groups at some point in life. We all are expected to dress and behave as the group demands. Peer pressure during adulthood may not be direct, but it challenges our core values. Forcing ourselves to behave like others and match others makes us lose self-control. This has a huge negative impact.

47. Sometimes we do not realize that we are doing certain things just out of peer pressure. What are the signs to recognize this?

At times, peers can contribute to a stressful life. Usually, peers communicate through subtle signals about following or doing things which might seem uncomfortable. Persons with low self-esteem tend to compromise, due to fear of rejection.

Peer pressure can be both positive and negative. Positive peer pressure helps to mould us into our best version.

SIGNS OF POSITIVE PEER INFLUENCE	SIGNS OF NEGATIVE PEER INFLUENCE
➢ Encouragement in performance like improving scores/grades ➢ Support when times are tough ➢ Accept the way we are ➢ Respect all our views	➢ Distractions from studies or performance ➢ Expecting others to change according to their comforts ➢ Force to indulge in risky behaviour ➢ Being secretive ➢ Motivates to break rules and avoid social situations ➢ Influence a drastic change in appearance

48. After recognizing this, it is a challenge to tell our friends an outright "NO" for the fear of being judged or labelled. In what other ways can "NO" be conveyed?

The feeling of belongingness comes when we are with persons who have similar choices in life. Finding one such person is a blessing. Being right and being on the right path is challenging in today's world. Saying "NO" for a wrong thing to a friend is not so easy because of the fear of being judged. But it is always good to remember that having good intentions, being right and decisive, empowers in saying "NO" easily. It is easier for confident individuals to be firm. In case we feel saying "NO" is hard, following others' choices (likes & dislikes) is even harder. Valuing our own feelings and beliefs, always directs us in doing the right thing. Refuse to please others at the expense of one's own emotional well-being. Setting boundaries for negative peer pressure is healthy. It helps to concentrate on things that are really important.

49. What is the best way to train children to prevent them from being swayed by peer pressure?

Children start caring more about friends as they grow up and try to fit in the group. Positive peer pressure is healthy and involves more encouragement and support. Negative peer pressure pushes them towards risky behaviour, which is unhealthy both mentally and physically.

SUGGESTIONS TO TRAIN CHILDREN ON HOW TO HANDLE PEER PRESSURE

- **Encourage children to be confident:** A confident child or a person handles pressure well. They know themselves better. They are not frightened or worried about others' approach.
- **Build their identity:** Let children know that they are loved and trusted. Help them know their strengths and weaknesses. They then start ignoring insults and labelling because they know themselves better.
- **Enabling children to make choices:** Encouraging children when they make healthy choices and teaching them that is OK to say "no" to things they don't want to do, is important.
- **Encourage them to follow rules:** Set family rules like:
    - No hurting
    - Waiting for their turn to speak
    - Using kind and polite words
    - Keep the room and house clean
    - By following rules ourselves, we set an example and also teach children acceptable and unacceptable behaviours.
- **Reinforce values:** Values or moral strength helps them to overcome challenges and stand up for core values.
- **Being expressive to seek support:** Seeking help is a positive step to reduce the impact of peer pressure. Talking to parents, mentors or friends who are facing similar challenges make them realize that it is common place and they are not the only ones facing such issues.

❑

Self Love
The Grey Zone

The concept of self-love is in the grey zone always. We have always been taught to put others ahead of us in everything. Anything that is done prioritizing our needs is considered to be a bad thing. It is not so always. Self-love is essential in many circumstances for protecting the self physically and mentally. However, excess of it does turn into selfishness. Both extremes are harmful. It is the balancing acts that will keep us stay centred.

50. Is self-love a synonym for selfishness?

Self-love is a simple concept but is of utmost significance. It indicates valuing and caring for our own needs, wants and desires. It is only when we can love our self in this manner; we can spend time and energy to be there for others. It is not about being selfish. Self-love to the extent required, is essential.

51. In day-to-day life and in the world around, we are always interacting with people most of the time. Where is the scope for self-love in such a scenario?

Practicing self-love does not mean taking out a scheduled time every day. It is not just about doing activities for self-care.

It is feeling good about ourselves and in all the things we do. It is about the feeling and not about the activity. Self-love also involves self-satisfaction and not seeking external validation. Amidst the hectic schedule, we can also combine self-care activities with routine work. For example: Listening to music while cooking. In short, every small activity that we do in a day can be done with self-love.

52. What are the different ways to integrate self-love into our daily routine?

Self-love can be practiced in many ways.

WAYS WE CAN LOVE OURSELVES NOW AND FOREVER

- **Stop all criticism:** Criticism never changes anything. Refuse self-criticism and turn it to self-acceptance. Everybody and everything is constantly changing. Self-criticism brings about negative changes while self-acceptance brings positive changes.
- **Self-compassion:** Let go of the past. At that moment, one would have done the best with the understanding, awareness and knowledge possessed.
- **Practise gratitude:** Gratitude is a high vibration that opens our hearts. Practise gratitude by being grateful for everything in life and in the world.
- **Be expressive:** We grow self-love when we express our feelings, needs and wants. Negative feelings dissolve and positive ones multiply.
- **Self-appreciation:** Our mind does not distinguish between appreciation from others or our own words or thoughts. Stop expecting appreciation from others.
- We all have been taught that placing oneself before others is selfishness. When will self-love turn into being too selfish or self-centered?

There is a very thin line between self-love and selfishness. Excess of self-love can convert into self-centeredness very fast if not checked in time.

53. We all have been taught that placing oneself before others is selfishness. When will self-love turn into being too selfish or self-centered?

There is a very thin line between self-love and selfishness. Excess of self-love can convert into self-centeredness very fast if not checked in time.

SELF-LOVE	SELFISHNESS
➢ Unconditional love towards self and others. This will be reflected in all actions, understanding others feelings and emotions better from their point of view. ➢ More of giving. ➢ Less demanding. ➢ Not attention seeking ➢ Setting healthy boundaries to protect self and others from resentment. ➢ Empathetic. ➢ Take responsibility in all actions and being flexible by considering everybody.	➢ Conditional love towards self and others meaning there is no consideration for others and their feelings. ➢ More of receiving. ➢ More demanding from self and others. ➢ Seeking attention most of the time. ➢ Lack of setting boundaries and violating others ➢ Lack of empathy. ➢ Escapes from daily chores, responsibilities, not flexible and end up hurting others. Controlling and manipulative.

54. What changes can be expected if we practice self-love?

- Self-love helps in making healthy choices in life. Example: Choosing a career which one really likes rather than the one which is trendy.
- Self-love helps to be helpful and empathetic.
- Self-love helps in prioritizing needs rather than wants.
- It also helps in practicing healthy life style by staying physically healthy, eating healthy and engaging in activities for the Self.

- Self-love enables self-appreciation and also appreciating others.
- It improves self-esteem, as the way we see, think and treat ourselves changes.
- It is easier to accept changes and take responsibility for all our actions. We treat every experience, success or failure as a learning curve.
- We feel less stressed when we go through challenges.
- Self-love increases resilience.

❑

Relationship

The Fairy Tale

Each one of us dreams of meeting a prince charming or a princess dazzling and wish for a happily ever after scenario in our lives. The dream is shattered only to realize that it is not easy to recreate a fairy tale in our mundane lives. Getting into, maintaining and managing a relationship successfully requires immense patience, effort and love from both the partners.

55. What is the measure of success in a relationship? Is spending a lifetime with a person indicator of a successful relationship?

A successful relationship can be shared between any two persons who respect, encourage and help each other grow, instead of constantly trying to be right. The idea of a perfect partner does not exist and no two persons are the same. Every relationship is unique. More than spending an entire lifetime or many years together, the important aspect is the manner in which it is spent. Standing by each other in all ups and downs, highs and lows of life is a better measure of success in a relationship rather than the number of years stuck together.

56. Sometimes each one of us feels, compromising or adjusting tantamount to losing our self-respect. Where should we draw the line while compromising or adjusting?

Relationships are complicated, delicate and one should be sensitive to know what to acknowledge and what to ignore. Compromise is part of a successful relationship and most of them require some sort of compromise. When one compromises with regard to any decision and if there is a feeling of being secure and connected, then it is a good compromise. Such a compromise is good for mental health. Hopefully it should be from both ends of the spectrum. If one feels that it is more one-sided, a problem has manifested and it needs to be revisited and re-evaluated. It is a signal indicating 'trouble' when one feels exhausted by decisions made and is forced to meet the partner's requirement by putting oneself down most of the time. This kind of compromise gives a feeling of being miserable and controlled. Despite the compromise one is made to feel as not being good enough. Constant put downs can affect the self-esteem which leads to feelings of anxiety. Unhealthy compromise creates an ever-expanding gap between partners and it is time to seek help together. Focus more on resolving the conflict respectfully.

57. "A stitch in time saves nine". Timely action sometimes can be a savior in many situations. When is it the right time to seek help in matters of relationship going off the track?

Red flags in a relationship:

- Lack of healthy communication
- Controlling behaviour
- Emotionally unavailable
- Argument on things that cannot be changed
- Frequent lying (constantly caught being dishonest)
- Active addiction

58. What is the 'key" to a successful relationship? How to ensure and maintain healthy relationships?

Relationships are formed from our life and our experiences. There is no one solution for all relationships as the idea of relationship is not the same for everyone. It also depends on the persons involved and the circumstances lived. However, few things remain as the basic foundation of a healthy relationship.

 **KEY TO HEALTHY RELATIONSHIPS**

- **Mutual understanding:** It is necessary to see through the eyes of the other person, identify the differences, understand it, accept and respect the differences. It is important to appreciate the similarities and respect the differences.

- **Communication:** There is a 'feeling of communication' when all needs, feelings, challenges, likes and dislikes are communicated to the partner.

- **Good listening:** Be a thoughtful, attentive and present listener whenever required.

- **Supporting each other:** As time passes, the needs, demands and priorities change. Be patient and support each other physically, mentally and emotionally.

- **Forgiveness:** Forget and forgive mistakes made in the past. Discussing the past and blaming pushes the partner away.

- **Spending time:** Spend time together. Despite the busy schedule, taking out time to do even small activities like exercising, shopping and doing household chores together matters.

- **Flexibility:** Being flexible and adaptable to meet the changing needs of the partner builds a strong relation.

❑

Parenting

Sculpting Life

Parents not only give birth and help raise a child; they in fact sculpt the child into a person. A person or personality has to be developed. Multiple factors shape an individual's personality and initially parents are the ones who shape and thus determine the future course of the child's development. This humungous task has to be done very consciously, bearing in mind that "As you sow, shall you reap".

59. Parenting is commonly viewed as just raising a child. It is considered as taking care of the child's physical and financial needs. What other things does parenting involve?

Parenting is not just about raising a child by taking care of a child's physical and financial needs. It is in fact a big responsibility, as it involves shaping a child into a healthy adult. This involves many more things than just supporting the child to grow in height or increase in weight or help them obtain educational degrees or a job. Parenting is the child's foundation for leading life and tackling its challenges in an efficient way. It is about channelizing children's thoughts, feelings and emotions in a crucible of a good value system so that the child can stride through life in the apt way.

60. How crucial is parenting in the child's transformation into a healthy individual?

Parenting is a major factor in influencing the development of a child. The quality of parenting is more essential than the quantity of time spent with the child. Early child development sets the foundation for learning, behaviour and health. It shapes the child's thinking and influences the future. Childhood indeed creates a strong base for the future. Childhood does not necessarily define a person, but it surely plays a great role. No matter how old we grow, there is always a child dwelling within each of us. It is very important to have a pleasant and healthy childhood. Unhealthy childhood might be the seed for the development of self-doubt, guilt, sense of inferiority, low self-confidence in the future, complexes and might sometimes also lead to self-isolation.

Making children's future colourful might be a challenging. But they deserve it. Children have never been good listeners to their parents. Never the less, they never fail to imitate them. Raising a child is one of the toughest and most fulfilling endeavours. Parents also learn along with the child.

61. One of the perspectives in parenting is that it is all about giving set of instructions to the child about dos and don'ts and shaping the child to be what the parents want them to be. Is this the right approach in parenting?

DO'S AND DON'TS OF PARENTING

DO'S

- **Be patient:** Everything is lost by losing temper. Actions speak louder than words. Every time, temper is lost and voice is raised against children, their anger response is being indirectly approved.

- **Ignore the behaviour of the child, not the child:** It is very important to always keep in mind that children's belief should be condemned and not them. It is better to tell "It is rude to push" than "You are rude". This ensures that children are not labelled. Labelling again has a huge impact on children. Children are open to receiving parents' comments. So, when children are called as "lazy", "fat", "stupid", "careless" etc. they believe it and will start living up to it. Positive labels like clever, thoughtful, brave and so on will reinforce good behaviour. For example: "I am really surprised to see you so angry".

- **Spend quality time:** Quality time is nothing but giving children undivided attention and doing tasks that they like to do. Initially, bedtime routine plays a crucial role. Quality time can be spent for some time when they wake up and when they go to bed. As they grow older, they will become independent. In the later years, it can be activities like doing yoga together, dinner, watching TV etc. Parents should shun gadgets for some time and just spend time listening and talking to children about their day.

- **Act immediately and be firm on values:** When a child breaks a rule or is not listening, correct them immediately. Do not wait for too long. Children may find it difficult to connect when it is explained at a later time regarding what was done a few days ago. They forget soon.

- **Appreciate:** Acknowledging children when they are right, appreciating with simple sentences such as "Good job" or by gestures like hugging, gives message to children that it is good to do such things again. As children crave for attention, they try to earn parents' praise repeatedly.

- **Approach:** Always communicate with children in a positive manner. For example: If we want children to be good listeners, we have to tell them that immense potential is already within them. The child just has to uncover the hidden potential.

DON'TS

- **Be a poor listener:** Please repeat what children tell or explain so they know that we are listening. Active listening makes them feel secure. They will receive feedback positively because they know that what they have narrated has been understood clearly.
- **Don't react:** Children are experts in picking up parents' triggers. Responding vs. reacting requires practice and it is challenging as well. Children tend to hide things and may start lying in apprehension of a reaction.
- **Don't break promises:** If a promise is broken, the child's trust is broken forever. It also makes them feel unimportant. Suppose a promise is broken for some reason, it is better to explain the reason and ask for forgiveness. Children learn from the actions/behaviour of their parents.
- **Don't Debate:** Be watchful about setting limits and end a healthy argument with discussion. If it oversteps the boundary, it is better to pause and discuss later.
- **Don't vent work pressure or frustration on children:** Remember children pine for their parents and long to meet them throughout the day. They deserve attention and by doing so, a feeling of compassion is nurtured in them.
- **Don't argue in front of children:** Children will observe and pick up certain things silently and this will have a dangerous impact on them throughout their life.

62. There is a notion that spending lot of time with children is a good thing to do. How much of time should we spend with children to be good parents?

In today's fast paced life, doing things in a slow manner is a huge challenge. In such a scenario, raising healthy and well-adjusted children can be even more challenging for parents due to lack of informal support from extended family and neighbors. The current competitive world is more demanding and both parents end up working day and night. This sometimes leads to an imbalance between family and work.

Spending time together is the foundation of a healthy family. It is important to spend quality time with children rather than estimating the duration. It is very crucial to pay undivided attention to children every day without fail. This special time with children strengthens the bond and helps parents know their children better. Good quality time with children will have a positive effect on them as they grow. By spending time with children, we are not only making memories for life, but also molding their future.

63. Every action has its consequences. What are the consequences if parenting is not done consciously?

Parenting should be done consciously as it comes with enormous responsibilities and should be done in a well-balanced manner. The style of parenting also plays an important role and has its own consequences. Paying excessive attention and getting involved in all of their activities or paying less attention and neglecting, both are poor parenting styles and impact children's' learning in different ways.

In the first scenario, where parents interfere in all the activities of their children and decide everything on behalf of the child like colour of the Tee Shirt, choice of friends, selection of toys etc.; children's decision-making skills and confidence levels are hampered. Involvement of parents in children's activities is appreciable, but affects children's creativity and their choices. Lack of decision-making ability is a huge deficit as these children grow into adults who fail to make independent decisions on important matters and depend on the opinions of others.

In the second scenario, where parents pay very less attention and do not know their children's activities like being unaware about their children's companions, eating habits, screen time, type of programmes they watch etc. fail to teach and correct them at the right time. Children get emotionally detached from parents as parents are not available for them, making way seek their emotional needs from other persons and in other relationships. This will be evident as children grow and consequences might be devastating in the long run.

IMPACT OF POOR PARENTING

- Low self-esteem
- Emotional and behavioral issues: Disobeying, aggressiveness, retorting, lying etc.
- Improper eating habits
- Sibling rivalry
- Resistance to studies
- Adjustment issues: Uncompromising attitude and not apologizing
- Tantrums
- Lack of responsibility and constantly blaming others
- Substance abuse, Addiction to gadgets

❑

Sibling Rivalry
The Cold War

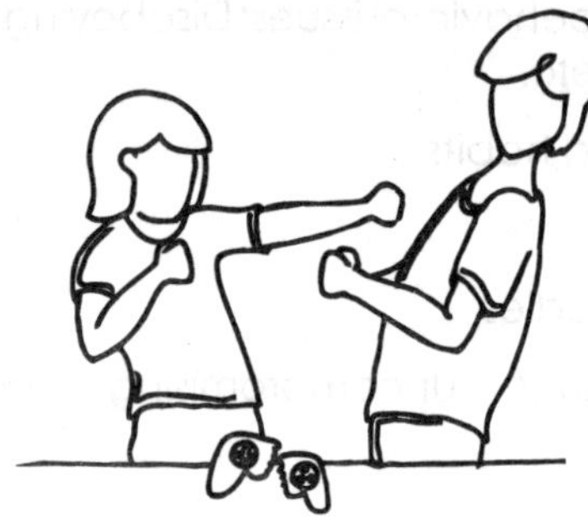

Siblings share a special bond and can become best friends for life, if a healthy bond is fostered between them. There are instances of enmity between siblings to unimaginable extents too. The blood relation and the bond become blurred and hazy in the backdrop of intense rivalry, the seeds of which are actually sown in childhood itself. Sibling rivalry should not be considered as something mundane as it can have disastrous consequences if ignored.

64. Each person plays a specific role in life, be it mother, father, elder, friend, teacher etc. What role does a sibling play in an individual's life?

Sibling is an everlasting relationship in most persons' lives. Siblings fill our life with good childhood memories which can be cherished always. Having a sibling is a boon. Siblings play a crucial role in shaping our life. They teach us sharing, caring, adjustment and compromise in life. Those with sibling/s have a better understanding of life and an added advantage of support-structure throughout life. No matter how strong the bonding is, there are no siblings who do not fight at all. Among the exhaustive list of fights between siblings, silly fights over the TV remote control, taunting each other, fighting over whose fault it actually was, throwing things at each other, blaming etc, are a few of the examples. These petty fights actually benefit in learning skills necessary to compromise and negotiate. But parents might be happy if their children do not fight among themselves. Not fighting with each other is also not a good sign as they usually end up not having a better understanding as adults. The sibling can be a source of support while unhealthy relationship with the sibling can be equally damaging.

65. In the past, joint families with a large family size was the norm. This gradually transformed into nuclear families with average family size of 3 to 4 (2 parents and 2 children). In the present times, most of the couples opt to have a single child. Is this a good trend then?

This is a debatable topic. The question is not about a single child. Much more important is the quality of parenthood. Creating a positive family balance is very important. Irrespective of the child having a sibling the best thing to do is to give the child quality time, love, support and a secured feeling.

Now, a single child norm is common for multiple reasons such as delayed parenthood, career goals, and financial constraints. Young couples prefer to give one child a better education and attention to provide the best possible lifestyle.

Having a single child or two children completely depends on family dynamics and how parents manage it. In order to handle such healthy challenges, before becoming a parent, the couple needs to educate itself on the roles and responsibilities of being a parent.

Before considering the decision to have a child, it is good to consider the following:

- Physically and mentally being willing to be a parent full time.
- Healthy and stable relationship between the couple.

- Financial stability
- Awareness about roles and responsibilities of a parent.

If the answer to all the above is an emphatic "YES", then the parents will be able to give their child the best possible. As a quote mentions, it is not necessary that one has to be rich to raise a child. But one needs to be wise.

66. Intention of the parents is always to give the best to their children. Then why does sibling rivalry set in? Is it due to the differences in children's perception?

None of the parents wish to see their children being jealous of each other, competitive and fighting all the time. More often than not, the impact of parenting style on sibling rivalry is more and more evident. Knowingly or unknowingly, parents tend to commit a few gross mistakes. So, we all should be aware about how sibling rivalry begins.

It starts right from the beginning of the second child's arrival. The attention is suddenly shifted from the elder one to the younger one. The elder one feels neglected followed by comparison. Some of the reasons that give rise to issues are praising one child to get things done and expecting elder ones to be smarter and understanding. Sibling rivalry may gradually lessen as they grow. If not handled properly, it will have a strong impact on their adulthood. The only need behind sibling rivalry is attention of the parent.

67. Growing up with siblings has lot of fun moments and a lot of fights in it too. There is nothing alarming about fights between siblings. When can be termed as rivalry?

Sibling rivalry is most common in families with two or more children and it is the way children compete for their parent's attention and love. Fights between siblings are common while growing up. But as they get older, their interaction too gets transformed. However, it is not the case always. Sometimes it does not change at all.

Red flags of Sibling rivalry :

- Not so welcoming about the new baby and the elder child shows anger by hitting, pinching or biting.
- Demands more attention from parents by crying and complaining of pains. Constant demand for attention when parents are busy with the other child.
- Increased verbal and physical fights as the siblings grow. Sometimes reacting in a higher level of violence.
- Regressive behaviour such as thumb sucking, bed wetting, baby talk etc. to imitate the younger one.
- Stops eating well or demands that parents should feed it.
- Mood swings due to stress, being easily tearful, temper tantrums and expressing frustration and anger against family members.
- Comparison in everything.
- Expects hand-holding in all activities.
- Calling each other names.
- Being selfish and refusing to share anything with the sibling.
- Never apologizes and regrets for the mistakes as they don't feel at fault.
- Not open to feedbacks and blame the parents for supporting the other child always.

68. How can parents handle sibling rivalry and foster a loving bond between them?

 **SUGGESTIONS TO HANDLE SIBLING RIVALRY**

- **Don't take sides:** It is natural to get upset when children fight. Avoid reacting and losing temper. Sometimes, no response is also a powerful response. Allow children to sort it out by themselves. Intervene only if necessary. Either child takes it the other way if parents try to figure out who is right or wrong. They forget about their actions and start the blame game, thinking that the parents always take sides.

- **Sharing:** In most families, younger siblings are encouraged or sometimes forced to use things that are used by elder siblings and they miss out on new things. Sometimes, elder ones will be more attached to their things which have to be forcibly shared or given to the younger ones. These kinds of situations make them feel jealous and resentful and are seeds for conflicts. They start seeing the other as a rival and competitor.

- **Pay individual attention:** Children behave inappropriately in order to seek attention from their parents. They consider attention as a reward for whatever is done. Show positive attention like smiling, eye contact, gentle physical touch and kind words whenever needed. Importantly, listen to them as per their needs. By doing so, trust and secure feelings are reinforced in them. It also helps them in building positive self-images.

- **Gender and Birth order:** First child of the family is given more attention than others. This is because parents are super excited about parenting and can be over protective and demand perfection from the child. Similarly, younger children are young forever. They are not taken seriously and they are not given responsibilities as well. Being the first born does not assure the same behaviour or treatment from parents. Boys are treated differently and given more importance in some cultures.

- **Big age gaps:** Few siblings with big age gaps take up more of a parenting role than being a sibling. Their childhood memories may be different from their friends. Sometimes, big age gaps can be helpful to the family as a whole. If the elder one is open, caring and welcoming, the scenario changes. The sudden change in life may sometimes give rise to sibling rivalry due to more attention given towards the younger one. It all depends on the dynamics of the family and parenting skills and the way everything is balanced. Now that parents are trained and have learned about parenting by bringing up the elder one, the first child might feel parents are calmer, relaxed and flexible.

- **Comparison in early childhood:** Each child is unique in its own way. Their skills and interests will rarely be the same. Generally, a child is always compared with its sibling right from developmental milestones like sitting, cradling, walking etc and also in looks. Comparing the elder one to the younger one in all these activities might point out towards one of them being slow. For example: one child starts walking at one year and younger child might have started walking at nine months. Every child grows and develops at a different pace. But when compared or judged in this manner, it hampers the child's development. Sometimes parents think the firstborn is more responsible and learns things faster. Parents fail to realize that the reason for this is that the older children are forced to learn to be prepared to welcome and manage small chores for the younger siblings. It's not the same for all families. It depends on parenting style. It is always a challenge to maintain balance. Parents should focus on the strengths of each child and highlight individual successes and make them realize that each one is the 'best' in its own way.

❑

Behaviour

A Person's Measure

The external appearance helps in identifying a person, but it is the behaviour by which a person is mostly gauged. Sometimes, the best looks will be redundant if behaviour is bad or inappropriate. It is a person's behaviour that ensures relationships are cordial. Often, we look in the mirror to check our appearance. It would do much good to us, if we hold a mirror to our behaviour as well, so that we can see what it reflects. Behaviour has its roots in the early stages of life. Those roots have to be planted with proper care in children, so as to yield appropriate behaviour. Plants can be bent, while trees cannot. Likewise unmodified early behavioural patterns will take concrete shapes and cannot be altered later.

69. Every word and action of ours reflects our behaviour. What are the indicators of good and bad behaviour?

Behaviour is communication. We all are communicating something thorough our behaviour during each moment of our life. When a child or adult is behaving inappropriately and in a problematic manner, it indicates that he or she is upset about something being wrong and that its needs are not being met.

When a child or adult's needs are not met in spite of repeated communication, they tend to use problem behaviour to seek attention and solution. When communication and purpose of children's behaviour are understood, any behaviour makes sense. Encouraging children's good behaviour is essential. Appreciate their behaviour and make them feel good by expressing happiness. By doing so, positive behaviour is reinforced and children also learn to repeat that behaviour to garner love and attention of their parents. Bad behaviour such as breaking rules, being disorganised, lacking hygiene, poor time management, watching television a lot reflects on failure of parenting and the inability to inculcate appropriate mannerisms in children. Bad behaviour is more in children with poor problem-solving skills and lack of knowledge. As parents, it is our responsibility to teach our children how to behave in an appropriate, respectful manner and deal with problems responsibly. Do not give up. You do not have that luxury. It is definitely hard at first and ultimately rewarding when things begin to change.

70. Behaviour is not acquired instantly or in a day. What influences behaviour?

The major influences on behaviour of the child are: the inherited traits, abilities they are born with, early childhood experiences and their day-to-day experiences. Sometimes children don't express their needs, but their behaviours do so. It is easy to make out the need of the child or adult if the behavioural patterns, the triggers and outcomes are closely observed and monitored. Please remember that the approach should always be positive. It does indeed matter a lot.

The other factors that influence behaviour are:

- **Lack of attention:** Lack of attention from parents can have negative consequences not only in childhood, but also in later stages of life. It affects them a lot. They try to seek the attention from others or from other places like problem behaviour in schools, with neighbours etc.

- **Lack of appreciation:** For children, parental attention is so powerful that whatever be the behaviour that is focussed upon, it will only increase. For example: We might be instructing children not to scream or back answer. But if they find out that it is the only way of reacting to them, it is their way of seizing our attention. To avoid such situations, focus more on dos and grab children's attention when they are being good and appreciate them.
- **Poor parenting:** There are certain parenting behaviours that can have serious negative effects on children and also on society like talking ill about others (gossiping), fighting in front of children, not respecting elders at home, complaining about elders at home and physical abuse. It can harm the child which leads to poor mental health. They learn a lot from our actions. They mirror us most of the time.
- **Lack of routines and inconsistency:** Routines help children to be well organised and gives them a sense of stability. It is important to adopt routines for the day like early morning, after school and bed time. These are specific times of the day that children need parents more and are most sensitive. To set a routine, as parents, we should follow it first.
- **Changes in family:** Situations like loss of loved ones, divorce and illness in the family are likely to modify children's behaviour. Sometimes, changing school or house can also have an impact on children's behaviour. Children feel disconnected and tend to behave inappropriately. Finding simple things to do together will help. Activities like going for a walk, exercising together, having a meal together etc.

71. Good behaviour is one of the finest pillars of character/ personality development. How can parents and teachers contribute towards good behaviour development among children?

The first mentors of the child are indeed parents followed by teachers. Both contribute a lot in shaping the child's personality. A child's age should determine the methods and ways that it should be taught. In other words it should be age appropriate. Teachers and parents should have mutual respect and support each other in the child's learning.

ROLE OF PARENTS AND TEACHERS IN BEHAVIOUR DEVELOPMENT

ROLE OF PARENTS

- Shower lots of love and affection
- Encourage good behaviour and give extra attention when you notice them doing something right.
- Be careful about your actions and words. They follow you.
- Be kind and firm when saying "NO". Please do make them understand the reason behind the "NO". They only understand things from their perspective and as per their age.
- Correct children immediately after the mistake or bad behaviour has occurred. Don't wait or postpone the correction or else children fail to connect.
- Be patient and don't nag about negative behaviour for a long time.
- Ignore the behaviour of the child, not the child.
- Avoid labelling, especially while teaching. They believe and trust parents a lot.
- Don't over punish.
- Spend quality time.
- Make them understand that, they have the freedom only to do the right thing.

ROLE OF TEACHERS

- Know all students well. Understand their learning styles, their aptitudes, interests and dislikes.
- Be consistent with rules.
- Use positive and kinder words.
- Be empathetic.
- Encourage children to express and participate.
- Get students' full attention before telling them something of importance.
- Be aware of your actions and body language.
- Every child is unique, be able to identify learning problems.
- Focus on the positives.
- Appreciate good behaviour.
- Don't insult them at any cost.
- Guide parents to seek help from a professional, if the child has learning disabilities or behavioural issues.
- Be approachable to children.

❑

Scholastic Performance

Genius Or Not?

Parents want their child to be a genius and the best performer in class is the teacher's favourite too. The cut-throat competition among students to secure 100% is intense and it is a virtual rat race to ascertain as to who is the best of the best. Most of the parents do not want to see their children falling short of the 'genius' mark even by a decimal. It is time to take a step back and contemplate whether performance in the examination means everything while children are lagging behind in learning and acquiring life skills. Students who are unable to reach the finishing line first are gently discouraged and slowly marginalised, as nobody has the patience and the time to deal with them. Parents and teachers should put in their combined efforts in the children's education so that they are guided appropriately.

72. In today's competitive world, education is mostly marks/ scores and is examination oriented. This decides the students' abilities. Is it the right way to assess the learning capacity of the students?

Marks and grades are recognition of hard work and performance in various exams. But it is only good as long as we are able to apply that knowledge to identify problems and find appropriate solutions. If not, then there is no use for grades and awards that are won. The present generation is focusing more on knowing. They do multiple courses, but fail to handle small challenges in real life. This trend gives rise to the question: what is the use of education or being called "qualified"? Knowledge gained earns value only when applied appropriately to resolve concerning issues. Children not only learn from the syllabi, but also from multiple sources like their experiences, peers, social media, teachers, family, role models and society at large. Just by scoring high grades, success is not assured. Success comes from a positive mental attitude, high skills and being creative. Sometimes, a bright or intelligent student may also underperform due to personal problems, health issues and trauma. It does not mean he or she is a failure. No method will completely capture the scope of a student's ability, unlike life. Given the right support and conditions, children's potential can be utilized to the maximum.

73. Sometimes teachers and parents label students as slow learners or as having specific learning disabilities. What is the impact of this on children?

Labels have the potential to damage young minds. Children grow and change, but the label unfortunately grows with them because it usually comes from trusted sources like parents, teachers and friends. This negatively affects the self-esteem which leads to self-limiting beliefs.

IMPACT OF LABELLLING ON CHILDREN

- Labelling can make children forget their true potential.
- By labelling repeatedly, children eventually start to believe it and act accordingly.
- When children are labelled, they are devalued and might miss out on the opportunities needed to reach their full potential.
- Labelling can actually influence the way others see and treat them.

- Positive labels create pressures on children to constantly perform well whereas negative labels limit their potential.
- Children fail to understand the importance of practice and hard work. They believe that the label cannot be changed.
- Children might start self-labelling.
- By constantly labelling, stress is created both in children as well as the parents.
- Social status of children is damaged.
- Children might have to deal with their peers making fun of them or bullying them.

74. What are the different kinds of labels?

Types of labelling:

• Name calling	• Shy
• Dumb	• Good
• Lazy	• Bad
• Worthless	• Intelligent
• Stupid	• Outgoing
• Tube light	• Weak
• Naughty	• Trouble maker
• Clever	

It is wise to think before speaking and choose the appropriate words.

75. Children are often playful and most of them do not like to sit down and study. This is the most commonly perceived reason for children not performing well in their studies. How can parents or teachers ascertain whether the child has learning disabilities or not?

Every child is unique and learns in different ways. The learning styles may vary. It could be visual (seeing), auditory (hearing) and kinaesthetic (doing). Children may find it difficult if the individual learning is not addressed. A child with learning disabilities may have difficulties in general comprehension, reading, writing, speaking, listening and understanding mathematical concepts.

A few signs of learning disabilities:

- Difficulty in pronouncing simple words.
- Difficulty in following instructions and need for repeated instructions.
- Difficulty in recognizing alphabets, numbers and words.
- Lacking in concentration.
- Difficulty in fine/gross motor skills like holding a pencil, tying shoe laces, buttoning the shirt etc.
- Difficulties in memorizing and poor memory on the whole.
- Lack of hand-eye co-ordination.
- Difficulty in remembering numbers and using correct signs for solving problems (using + instead of -).
- Difficulty in reading and writing.
- Difficulty in grasping new skills.
- Difficulty in copying or reverses the alphabets.
- Struggles to get organized.
- Trouble telling the time.

Please note that it is necessary to rule out vision, hearing and any developmental issues that cloud the underlying learning disability. Consult a psychologist and seek professional help for further evaluation.

76. What are the types of learning disabilities that we can encounter in children?

The different types of learning disabilities are:

- **Dyslexia:** Difficulty processing language- issues in reading, writing and spelling.

- **Dyscalculia:** Difficulty with mathematics – problem solving, mathematical sums, understanding concepts with numbers, time and money.
- **Dysgraphia:** Difficulty in writing- difficulty with handwriting, spelling and organizing ideas.
- **Dyspraxia:** Difficulty with fine motor skills- problems with hand-eye co-ordination and balance.
- **Auditory processing disorder:** Difficulty in hearing differences between sounds- problem with reading, comprehension and language.
- **Visual processing disorder:** Difficulty in interpreting visual information like difficulty in reading maps, charts and symbols.

77. How can children with any of the learning disabilities be trained further? What is the right approach?

TRAINING CHILDREN WITH LEARNING DISABILITIES

- First and foremost, parents and teachers should educate themselves regarding all the aspects concerning learning disabilities. This familiarity with the subject will help them support the child in dealing with all those
- multi-pronged challenges that it has to face daily, without getting discouraged at any point in time.
- Getting updated regarding new research and findings in learning disability and education techniques.
- Identify the child's learning style and use that to teach it at school and at home.
- Children with learning disabilities require individual attention which includes specific, directed and individualized remedial instructions.
- Go in for small goals and provide intense practice.
- Use pictures, videos and diagrams to teach them.

- Provide direct and simple instructions.
- Encourage students to ask questions.
- Avoid distractions in class.
- Point out unfamiliar words and explore their meaning.
- Allow extra time if necessary while reading or writing.
- Present activities that involve all sensory modalities.
- Arrange for peer help to share notes and discuss the subject at hand.
- Use colours to grab their attention.
- Use different formats to teach the same concepts.
- Revise to reinforce learning.
- Teach memory retention techniques.
- Be specific while giving instructions.
- Be patient and kind and generous.
- Encourage them to seek help whenever needed.

78. Parents and teachers play a very crucial role in children's education. How should each one contribute to their academic Performance?

A child's academic performance will be better, healthier and productive only when parents and teachers work hand-in-glove and aim for the best. A balance between school and home learning plays a key role in moulding the students.

GUIDE TO AID CHILDRENS ACADEMIC PERFORMANCE:

- **Healthy parent and teacher relationship:** Children play a different role in school. Know children from the teachers' perspective too and make sure to correct them if need be. Don't miss the interaction sessions and meetings at the school. Children feel good when they see their parents and teachers being friendly and cordial with each other.

- **Prioritize children's learning:** Be regular. Don't encourage children to take unnecessary leave from school for attending ceremonies, trips and other trivial and silly reasons. Teach them to be committed and prioritize what is important. This is learnt by children effectively when we follow the same.

- **Be a good listener:** Encourage children to share about what is happening in school and with friends. Make them feel like they are being supported at all times.

- **Convey positive attitude towards teachers or parents:** This applies to both teachers and parents. Don't bad mouth about each other in front of children. Children will lose trust and in turn will lose interest in studies as a result.

- **Work together:** Though parents know their children very well, the teacher knows them better as students. Be open to feedbacks from teachers and if the same issue persists at home, then as a team, make a plan and work together to make it consistent across environments.

- **Avoid over-scheduling:** Play is equally important. Unlike learning, don't burden them by over scheduling extra learning activities. Play time and rest time is very important to have a memorable childhood.

- **Positive criticism:** If children are not performing well or show lack of interest in studies, correct them immediately. Make them understand as to what is right and what is wrong. Avoid ill words and blaming and shaming them.

- **Reward them for results:** Always compare children's results with their previous results and not with their friends or neighbours' results. However, do not over shower them with gifts for an average performance too.

- **Know children's strength:** It is natural to focus on things that are not going well for our children. But it is important to follow children's interest too. It helps children build self-esteem. Talking about their strengths can help both.

- **Be slow, steady and consistent:** Don't expect everything to change overnight. Try to match children's speed after ascertaining their learning abilities and speed. Encourage them to improve. Moving too fast actually makes learning take longer time.

If none of these methods work, then it indicates that it is time to seek help from a professional.

❑

A Sudden Twist In The Tale

The Covid Pandemic

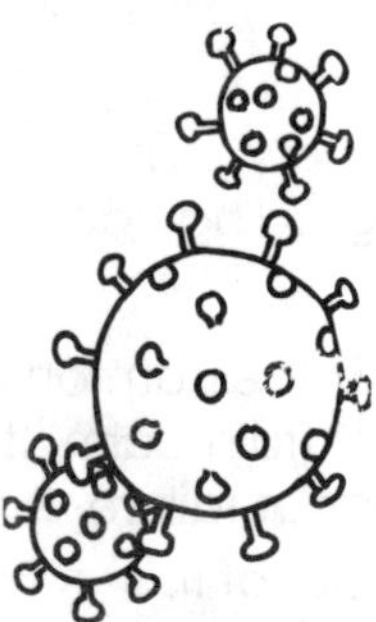

The Covid-19 pandemic was a sudden assault on the entire world. It's as if a button was pushed and the whole world came to a standstill in terms of flow in all sectors and spheres of life. It was a question of life and death to many and nothing else mattered. There were sudden changes overnight with uncertainties everywhere. It was indeed like staring at a blank wall. This was a test of resilience for everybody. This pandemic exposed the impact of unhealthy lifestyles, behaviours and thus a lack of resilience. Stress, anxiety and depression emerged as bigger burdens as and how the pandemic progressed. The lesson learnt is to be prepared rather than getting ready after the inevitable has struck.

79. Covid-19 pandemic brought about a lot of changes globally not just in terms of health, but also challenges in all aspects of life, personal and professional. Adjusting to the new scenario is a difficult task for most of us. Why did this happen?

The only 'constant' in life is change. – HERACLITUS

Familiarity gives everyone a feeling of safety. But life is all about change. Knowingly or unknowingly, we are constantly changing.

Nothing is fixed. None of them feel the same as the day before. None of them are with the same thought processes at all times. Each one's state of mind, looks, likes and dislikes are constantly changing. There is no growth without change. Everything around us is also changing, be it nature (day, night, seasons), body, thoughts, plants and animals. Yet, we fail to learn and accept change because of the following:

- Fear of the unknown or trying something new and losing things.
- High risk: Trying out new things involves high risk. It also increases anxiety regarding facing uncertain results and situations.
- Feels secure and safe in the comfort zone: Being in a comfort zone always helps maintain calm. It also involves less effort, no anxiety and no fear of failure. It might be very hard and challenging to come out of it.

80. How to make ourselves more adaptable and resilient so that we adjust to challenges quicker?

Stepping out of the comfort zone will definitely help us find many opportunities. The way the opportunities are utilized matters the most.

 **DEVELOPING RESILIENCE**

- **Be open minded:** Be open minded and take risks. Avoid comforting behaviour that holds back from exploring new opportunities. Strongly decide to step forward into growth which in turn helps to learn new skills and cope with new challenges.
- **Adaptability and flexibility:** Be flexible in all situations and circumstances. Adaptability enhances strength. Facing challenges also unlocks the doors to happiness. Initially it might be time consuming and energy exhausting. Sometimes setbacks are also common and others' help might be required. But eventually everything will bounce back to normal.

- **Problem solving skills:** Practice creative problem solving and enhance problem solving skills. **Emotional stability:** Learn to control and handle emotions with ease and confidence.

- **Reframe thoughts:** Stop viewing change as a threat and start looking at it as an opportunity to learn and grow.

- **Get support:** Reach out to others who are facing challenges and get their support. This helps to cope with change in an efficient manner.

- **Socialize:** All of us at some point in time feel lonely when facing challenges. Avoid making excuses to maintain an idealistic self–image. Stay physically active and connected with persons around. Interact with those who share common interests and values. If loneliness persists, please seek professional help.

81. Covid-19 pandemic set in a new normal in 'Work From Home' (WFH) for adults and online schooling for children. The lines between personal and professional work is blurred. How to achieve work-life balance?

The pandemic has brought about a drastic change all across the world. All of us were forced to adjust to new changes like online classes, working from home and lack of socialization. Work-life balance is very important, whether it is work from home or going to the office.

 **TIPS TO ACHEIVE WORK-LIFE BALANCE**

- **Designate space for work:** Home office or designated space should only be used for office work. Avoid using that space for other activities. By doing so, there will be more productivity as there would be no distractions.

- **Set boundaries:** Set the duration for working hours. Stick on to the 'log in' and 'log off' timings. Try to focus on other activities like spending time with family and friends, exercises or other physical activities to stay healthy.

- **Be aware of screen time:** Avoid checking emails, notifications and updates while starting and ending the day. Walk out from the work space, once the work timing is over. Screen free time with family helps better relaxation.
- **Indulge in self-care activities:** When we are able to take care of ourselves well, we are less susceptible to respond negatively to challenges. It also reduces stress and anxiety.
- **Ask for help:** If there are issues like thought rush, feeling low most of the times or feeling extremely stressed out, it is time to seek help from friends, family or a psychologist as they can reveal newer perspectives.

82. How to guide children to adjust to this scenario?

Due to the pandemic, we all are facing challenges and changes which no doubt make us experience a sudden shift in all aspects of life. Children probably don't understand the reason behind such a huge change. In such conditions, the following tips can help:

GUIDE TO HELP CHILDREN ADJUST TO THE NEW SCENARIO

- **Maintain a daily routine:** Maintaining a regular routine gives a sense of control and well-being. Sudden disturbance in all sectors of life can make life more stressful. Regularity is very challenging, while facing tough times. But it helps to bounce back to normalcy faster.
- **Practice and teach:** Children tend to look up to adults for help and guidance. They learn from adults on how to handle stress and challenges. Demonstrate how to engage in positive behaviour and practices.
- **Educate them about new normal:** Teach them about self-care to promote safe behaviour such as wearing face masks, maintaining hand hygiene and social distancing. Also discuss about the changes happening and keep them updated.

☞

- **Limit screen time:** Due to online classes children spend more time in front of the screen and on the other hand, many parents also use screens to keep the child engaged while they are attending other needs. Children are exposed to boredom. They relax more on screen. This leads to lack of self-control. Use screen only when work demands or as needed.

- **Encourage social skills:** Children have mostly been at home without any outdoor games during the lockdown. They have also not been sent out to play due to parental concerns regarding Covid-19 infection. Children learn more through play and interactions with peer groups. In such scenarios, provide them with virtual options, to engage in healthy social interactions. Overdoing any activity, at any cost, is not advised.

83. During the pandemic, many lost their loved ones to Covid-19 and it was sudden and unpredictable. How to cope with the sudden void and deal with this traumatic situation?

Grief is a difficult and natural response. We all are a part of the collective grief by losing something now. Some of them lost their loved ones, some lost their jobs. Children lost their freedom, school time, play time and the list goes on and on. But the death of loved ones in this pandemic has an enormous impact, due to multiple reasons such as:

- Family members were unable to be with their loved ones because of the Covid-19 pandemic and infection control restrictions.

- They failed to see them in their final stages and perform the last rites.

- Lack of family support during this time as there was no consoling or sharing the grief. The reason being that many could not travel due to the restrictions placed.

Since there was no physical interaction, the situation became even more challenging. But all said and done, life has to move on and everybody has to bounce back to normalcy, so that the dependants don't suffer. Help has to be rendered to them to cope with all the trauma and grief too.

COPING UP WITH SUDDEN TRAUMA

- **Acceptance:** It is important to accept the reality and try to restore our well-being. Being in denial for a long time delays the recovery and prolongs the grief and suffering, which is unhealthy.
- **Expressing feelings:** Share feelings with friends and family. This helps in venting out then and there without adding to the already existing baggage. Expressing feelings heals.
- **Avoid over thinking:** Don't over think and stop imagining the different ways it could have happened. Don't self-criticise or blame others for whatever has happened. Try to understand that the situation is new and challenging to everyone.
- **Socialize:** Avoid spending time alone. Spend time with friends and family as this will divert the attention and keep the mind occupied with other things. Engage in activities which help relax both body and mind. It is very important to keep in mind that just sticking to rigid social conditions about handling grief as per societal constructs like avoiding social gatherings is more damaging, as it reinforces suppression.
- **Have faith:** Avoid thoughts like protesting death, losing faith in Self, others and God. Find joy and satisfaction in life.

❑

Crossing Boundaries

Mental Health In Physical Illnesses

In major physical health illnesses or disease conditions, especially those requiring long term medical and rehabilitative treatment, impact on the mental health is equally worrisome, as it is to the physical body. Addressing mental health issues in such scenarios will drastically improve response to treatments and the outcome too

CANCER

84. The moment we hear the word 'Cancer' we feel like it is the end of the world. How to cope with a diagnosis of cancer?

A cancer diagnosis is blindsiding and can have a tremendous impact on the person's mental health. It affects physical, mental, social and spiritual aspects of life. The word 'cancer' is always related to end of life scenarios. The moment the diagnosis is communicated by the doctor to the patient; there might be a sudden rush of thoughts with an inability to think clearly. There may be a sudden surge of feelings of helplessness and anxiety about the future. There arises questions, "why me?" "Why only me"? It is quite natural to feel so. This happens due to a sudden deviation of life. Added to this, incorrect information, mindless browsing and spiced-up dreadful stories shared by friends, colleagues and relatives accentuate these feelings. Few other worries would also include body image issues, family concerns and financial issues including paying treatment expenses.

DEALING WITH FEAR ON DIAGNOSIS:

- Learn/know the facts from a genuine source i.e., the treating doctor and clarify all the doubts.
- Be open. Don't suppress emotions. Talk to near and dear ones.
- Try to maintain a normal routine and also be flexible as to modify it as and when necessary.
- Be open to seek help physically and psychologically.
- Plan finances for the treatment.
- Talk to persons who have been in a similar situation (cancer survivors). Their positive inputs will help motivate.
- Don't restrain from doing anything just because of the cancer diagnosis.
- Stop blaming or self-criticising and look for reasons to have hope for a positive future.
- Focus more on what you can control.
- Don't compare with other patients, as each patient is different. No two patients are the same as a lot of factors vary, like age, body weight, clinical presentation, co-morbidities etc). Don't define your health looking at other patients.

Always remember, every thought is powerful and has its impact on the body and mind. Stop imagining negative possibilities.

It is good to slow down. This brings awareness regarding what resonates with us and what does not. This helps us to live in the present moment and focus entirely on that particular moment. This in turn brings a good shift in life. A habitual practice is to always question the external factors, especially when we face adverse circumstances. Instead, self-introspection will help find answers from within.

Example: Why do I feel angry when I think of my illness? This helps you understand your need/self better.

85. Duration of cancer treatment is variable depending on various factors. Irrespective of the duration, there are a lot of concerns the patient has while undergoing treatment. How to deal with them?

A small meeting between the healthcare team and family will help in deciding about the choice of treatment. It is important to be open in a discussion and clarify everything regarding frequency of hospital visits and therapy sessions, duration and cost of treatment, benefits of treatment and its side effects. This ensures clarity in the healthcare team, patient and the family.

Once an informed choice is made and treatment begins, few changes can be expected physically and mentally. At the same time, there can also be changes in family roles as priorities change.

Some of the modalities of cancer treatment are surgery, chemotherapy and radiotherapy. Treatment involves several sessions ranging from few months to years and might also have some unpleasant side effects. Every patient does not get all the side effects and to the same degree. But many get a few of them. Dealing with them depends on the issue being faced and can be dealt appropriately. One of the most common side effects of treatment is hair fall or loss and is the most challenging as it is related to the body image. Females find it more challenging than males. In most of the instances, hair will begin to grow back after chemotherapy is done. This may take two to three months. Options to deal with it can be either choosing to cover the head with a wig or scarf or not wanting to cover it at all. Choose the most comfortable option.

As energy levels keep changing, be open to seek help from family and friends to do household chores. By doing so, they also feel good and it also prevents caregiver burn outs. Don't have many plans while getting treatment. Give priority only to the most important activities. Practice relaxation techniques and stay occupied with activities that

De-stress the bodymind. Eat healthy food, drink plenty of fluids and get adequate rest to manage fatigue due to the treatments. Dealing with cancer as a disease affects the patient, the whole family and the circle of friends. So be honest and express all needs and feelings with beloved ones. By doing so, mutual support is enhanced. Try to maintain normal routine. It is very beneficial for both physical and emotional recovery. Talk to persons dealing with similar situations. This brings newer insights in dealing with challenges during the treatment process. Sometimes, one may feel overwhelmed and may indeed feel like talking to someone outside the inner circle for support. Feel free to express feelings of fear, anger or sadness and consult a psychologist for counselling. They will encourage the patient to open up and talk about issues which are bothersome, in order to address the root cause and help find better ways of coping.

86. We have heard stories of cancer survivors who have overcome their difficulties with sheer will power and determination. How to inculcate this mindset with a positive outlook?

DEVELOPING A POSITIVE OUTLOOK

- **Optimistic attitude:** An optimistic attitude definitely helps one cope easily with any kind of illness. Life is all about facing unexpected events and challenges. But what brings a change is the way it is faced head on.

- **Expressing emotions:** It is OK to vent out feelings of anger, fear and suppression with loved ones. Expressing emotions will help face life better. It is very difficult for friends and family to understand the feeling of dealing with something as grave as cancer, unless they have experienced a similar situation before.

- **Reframing thought patterns:** In order to overcome any challenge of life, we first need to shift our thoughts from denial (why me) to acceptance (what next). Once the problem is accepted, change begins. Reframe thoughts in a way that it gives a good feeling and a good vibe. Avoid triggering stress by focussing on the negative parts of day. It is important to be cautious not to dwell on the same thoughts over and over again.

- **Interaction with near ones:** Interact with persons who reinforce good thoughts and who bring smiles on the face. A smile, simple touch, gentle hug and caring words from loved ones make a huge difference. Remain honest in confronting fears and concerns. This will enable managing the situation well.

- **Engaging in activities:** Do things and activities which are enjoyable and boosts the energy levels.

- **Gratitude:** There are ups and downs, pain and pleasure in everybody's life. Please focus more on blessings and stop complaining. By doing so, the quality of life is enhanced.

- **Flexibility and Adaptability:** Be flexible and adaptable to change. This allows in the development of new skills and new ways of dealing with life at all levels. Each of these small actions adds up to the accomplishment.

- **Self-belief:** Lastly, self- belief will work wonders in resolving all conflicts and crises.

- **Seek help:** Never feel lonely. Seek help whenever needed.

87. In end-of-life stages or scenarios, what is the right approach of thinking and decision making for the patient and the care givers?

When it comes to end of life phase, it is natural to feel anxious, panicky, guilty, anger and also feel very lonely and abandoned. This is because many avoid discussing death for a multiple number of reasons such as:

- Fear of Death
- Death does not sound positive
- The assumption that death happens only to the aged. By doing so, it is just ignoring reality that life is full of uncertainties.

Nobody including the doctors can predict the exact amount time that an individual may survive. In comparison to sudden death, getting to know that, the time of death might be nearing, has advantages. It gives time to prepare for it, to arrange help for dependants or family members, to forget certain issues, to forgive those around you and to express everything unsaid. In one word, you get time to be healed and acquire a sense of peace and calm. The topic of death might seem like an uncomfortable one and may induce feelings of negativity. But giving a thought to death actually helps all in reflecting about values and the purpose of life. At this point of time, the caregiver plays a very crucial role.

As a caregiver, it is important to let the person on the death bed know that they are precious and loved through words and actions. Express love by giving gentle hugs, paying more attention to their needs. Be an active listener as they might have a lot to speak about their pain and fear. Sometimes, they may become silent or may avoid conversing totally. Help them to keep themselves clean and comfortable. Openly share feelings and remain empathetic to the situation. Encourage them to pray and thank daily. This brings out the best for them physically and spiritually.

LONG TERM HEALTH ISSUES LIKE DIABETES AND HYPERTENSION

88. A diagnosis of hypertension (high blood pressure) and diabetes (high blood sugar) indicates being hooked on to medicines for a lifetime. This makes one feel anxious. How to deal with this kind anxiety?

As medical conditions such as diabetes and hypertension require being on treatment modalities throughout life, it is absolutely normal to feel anxious, shocked, confused and low for the few days after the diagnosis has been done. It will take some time to overcome the initial feelings and adopt the new everyday challenges associated with the condition. No matter the challenge, the typical reaction initially is denial (why me?). It is always good not to get stuck in denying facts. The way out of any problem is always seen when it is accepted. Constant stress for any reason can affect mental and physical health. It increases feelings of restlessness, irritability, de-motivation and isolation.

 **Here are some suggestions to help deal with anxiety:**

- **Self-care behaviour:** Focus on more of self-care behaviour by complying with doctor's instructions and treatment protocol, initiating the necessary lifestyle changes for good health and being careful about protecting health at all costs.

- **Stress reduction measures:** Practice relaxation techniques, share feelings with friends, family and trusted ones. Talk to the healthcare team to clarify doubts if any. Stay occupied by doing activities that aid relaxation. By reducing stress, the mind is free of worries and also it is easier to manage health issues and challenges.

- **Seek help:** Seek help at the right time if stress and anxiety get out of hand.

89. Diseases with a long duration will have lot of titrations in dosage of medicines and treatment protocol. Sometimes, it feels like being dependent on medicines for living more than food itself. This makes it so depressing to live life in such a manner. What can be done to overcome these feelings in such situations?

Fluctuations in health in long standing conditions might cause fear and anxiety. Apart from medical reasons for the fluctuations in such cases, some of the reasons which increase stress and anxiety in such scenarios are:

- Focusing more on unhealthy behavior and thoughts which reinforce it further and increase stress.
- Lack of motivation to keep up with lifestyle changes such as diet and exercise and relying on medicines as an easy way to tackle the challenges.
- Comparison with friends and family with similar health issues and making self-assumptions about the course of the disease.

SOME TIPS TO HANDLE STRESS IN SUCH SCENARIOS

- **Self-motivation:** Stay self-motivated to adhere and continue the intake of medicines, maintain life style measures such as diet, exercise and rest as advised.
- **Be in the present:** Be in the present moment and don't get anxious about the future.
- **Stop comparing:** Comparing nurtures unnecessary fear and it is best to avoid comparison of any kind.
- **Change the mindset:** Commonly most of them relate medicines to sickness only. Instead, if the mindset is changed and it is related to becoming healthy, it does wonders.
- **Positive affirmations:** Repeating positive affirmations like: "I am always healthy and always feeling healthy" reinforce positive thought patterns in the subconscious mind. ☞

- **Self-control:** Practice self-control and focus on those aspects that can be controlled at an individual level. Stop trying to control external factors.

90. How can individuals with hypertension and diabetes make use of power of the mind to maintain optimal quality of living?

Mind power is the strongest and subtlest power we all possess. This power has the capacity to create anything we focus on. The object and direction of focus matters a lot. It is good if the focus is on success, happiness and opportunities. Instead, if we get stuck to "what if" questions, it drains energy, causing stress and we end up attracting the same. Thoughts have a very subtle power and can affect reality. Not all thoughts have an impact on reality, but the predominant thoughts do so. Hence, it is important to be extremely cautious regarding investing of our thought power.

 **UNLOCKING THE MIND FOR BETTER SELF-UNDERSTANDING**

- **Inculcate positive thinking:** Positive thinking does not mean that we stop paying attention to negative feelings and experiences or totally ignore them. Instead, positive thinking means there is acceptance about the happenings in life and believe that whatever happens is for the highest good in life. Any situation in life does not pull anybody up or down. Ups and downs are caused by the way it is perceived and approached.

- **Reinforce only positive beliefs:** As already mentioned, energy flows towards the object of focus. Thus, it is very important to reinforce only positive beliefs. Self-introspection helps in identifying self-critical and negative self-talk like "I am always sick", "I am not strong enough" etc. Such damaging beliefs need to be changed to the belief that "I am strong and healthy", "I am happy" etc. ☞

- **Having a strong intention to heal:** We have the power to change reality by using our thoughts and powerful intention. Nurture good intentions and have strong will power to create anything as per wishes.
- **Being surrounded by good company:** The persons whom we spend time with or the company we keep is pivotal, as there is mutual influence of thoughts, decisions and choices. Thus, staying surrounded by persons with optimistic attitudes will make a huge difference.
- **Visualisation:** Constantly visualizing whatever we want in life helps in manifesting it. This is possible as the subconscious mind accepts the imagination as real and cannot distinguish between reality and imagination.
- **Be in the present:** Our mind always dwells in the past or in the future and we spend very less time in the present. Spend most of the time in the present and focus on one thing at a time. Productivity and efficiency increase when we are fully engaged in one task at a time. It also makes us feel calm and relaxed.
- **Practice gratitude:** Being thankful to everything in life will shift attention from complaining, to being grateful, from scarcity to abundance. A small exercise to practice this on a daily basis will bring in significant change. Close the eyes and thank at least three things in life in the present moment.
- **Practice forgiveness:** Forgiveness helps by consciously releasing feelings of resentment towards a person or a group, irrespective of whether they deserve it or not. By forgiving others, we allow ourselves to overcome feelings of anger, bitterness or revenge. Unresolved conflicts can go deeper and affect physical health too. It also opens the path and gives the opportunity to live in the moment.
- **Flexible mindset:** A flexible mindset enhances well-being of both the body and mind. It moves us from self-limiting thought patterns towards possibilities. It assists in adapting to changes easily. Fixed mindset is self-limiting and induces feelings of insecurities and being threatened by others' success, problems etc. A flexible mindset releases us from this prison of self-limiting beliefs.

- **Mindfulness practices:** Mindfulness practices like yoga, meditation, pranayama, vipassana etc help to reduce stress and anxiety. It shifts our attention from suppressed emotions to emotional well-being. It also helps boost attention, concentration and eventually improves the core quality of life.

PSYCHO-SOMATIC ISSUES

91. Body aches, joints pain are common complaints faced by many. Sometimes, all medical reports are normal. Yet, the aches and pains persist and doctors advise the patients to seek professional help for the stress. Why does this occur? How is stress affecting the body?

There are certain mental health issues which causes vague body aches accompanied by fatigue, sleep disturbances and mood swings. Many often complain about these symptoms after an event of physical trauma like surgery, abusive relationship, death of loved ones, divorce etc. Women are more affected than men. In traumatic and intensely stressful situations in life, as a normal response to the stressors, the body and mind undergo some definitive changes. Stress can be beneficial to health in short term situations and is a natural part of our fast-moving lives. Persistent stress for a long duration is harmful for both mental and physical health. The body and mind are inter-related and this often goes unrecognised. Each and every word, thought and action affects the body. The body receives them without judgement, irrespective of whether it is positive or negative. This results in effecting the body. Frequent and repeated thoughts or contemplation about a specific issue will increase stress and will also present as issues affecting the body. For example: worrying excessively about a professional matter or discussion pertaining to a job might result in headache and anything that triggers discussion about the job, will in turn trigger the headache. Likewise, various causes that have stressed the individual go out of control, can manifest as medically unexplained body pains, joint aches, fatigue, brain fog, etc. Individuals, who complain repeatedly, blame and nag also can be seen with these symptoms.

92. What measures should we take to prevent recurrence of these kinds of body aches, pains and fatigue?

At the outset, to tackle the complaints, a combination of therapies like medicines to alleviate pain, psychotherapy and self-care strategies will help a lot.

Self-care is very important and plays an important role in prevention of recurrent aches and pains. Many of us forget to take care of ourselves due to many other responsibilities in life. Handling stress becomes more challenging, when we are physically and mentally exhausted. We become more resilient to handle stress, when we feel good both physically and emotionally.

FEW TIPS TO TUNE THE BODY AND MIND

- **Stay physically active:** Regular exercise in almost any form boosts the energy levels, keeps worries away and gives a sense of general well-being. Persons who are physically active have better mental health.

- **Socialize:** Social interactions help generate dopamine (happy hormone) which gives a good feel and fights pain. Talk to those around and make good friends. Walking or exercising with a partner keeps up the motivation, makes it more fun and is more effective.

- **Maintain a healthy lifestyle:** Handling stress becomes easy when a good lifestyle is followed. Eating a healthy diet is a key to decrease stress. Try not to skip meals or eat on the run. Relax and enjoy the food. How the food is eaten matters a lot. Avoid caffeine and alcohol.

- **Improve sleep quality:** Poor sleep and sleeping overtime, both trigger the symptoms. Adequate amount of rest each night is essential for everyone to lead a healthy life. Set up a sleep schedule, go to bed and get up at the same time every day. It helps in body restoration.

- **Awareness and attention:** Awareness and clarity about the problem itself will solve half of the problem. This will also make us cautious about paying attention to only necessary and essential things. Identifying the stressors will help in arriving at the correct solution. Even in instances where we fail to know the solution, learning from past experiences and failures will ensure that those experiences are not repeated.

- **Listen to the body:** Getting tuned to the needs of the body will prevent certain experiences from recurring. In cases of extreme stress or in situations whenever the body signals that certain situations are triggering stressful responses in the body, it is important to listen to the body and not get indulged in it.

- **Developing resilience:** Resilience will help in accepting and adapting to challenges a faster rate. This is with an approach towards seeking solutions, by focussing on things which are under our control. If not, the focus will be on things which are not in our control and the complaining will be in vain.

- **Seek help:** Meet a counsellor or a medical professional to overcome the symptoms. Learn relaxation and mindfulness techniques to maintain daily functioning positively. It also helps to accept the feelings as they are and take action based on personal values.

❑

The Moral Compass

Role Of Values In Mental Health

A moral compass present within each of us indicates the direction while navigating through life, to ascertain whether we are on the right path or not. It is up to us to pay heed to it or ignore it. Following the right path may not always be easy. It has its own challenges and may seem like hard testing times. The victorious ones are the ones who stick to their core values and ethics no matter what life throws at them. Value-based living brings satisfaction, peace and contentment in life. These promote good mental health. Lack of core values add on to the baggage of negative emotions like guilt, shame, deceit etc. These ruin mental health over a period of time.

93. Stories with focus on values and morals have been passed down generations and have been taught by parents, teachers and elders in the family or clan. They are generally viewed as codes of conduct to guide the individual in his day-to-day life. Does it have a role to play in mental health?

Yes, certainly, stories remain as an all-time favourite for all age groups and it is the most powerful means to influence, teach and inspire everybody. Stories are easy to grasp and remember. It also connects us to the ancient traditions and helps us learn the values and purpose of life or certain universal truths. Imagination is triggered when you are actively listening to a story and is processed in the brain as though they are real experiences. Value-based stories help an individual to raise self-esteem and take responsibility for their individual actions. It also helps us discriminate between good and bad and right and wrong. It encourages them to think critically about their actions and its impact on themselves and others. It enhances and helps us imbibe values to overcome personal challenges.

94. How do following values and morals help in maintaining good mental health? (conscience, truthfulness, honesty, justice, compassion, etc.)

Values and morals keep us grounded and help us lead a clean and meaningful life. But following values and morals is not easy. It takes tremendous patience and effort to make it happen. But surely it is worth it. We live in a society that overemphasizes 'perfection' and 'successes. We are always racing, stressing ourselves, deciding on 'do's' and 'don'ts'. When we follow our values, the choices become easy and there is clarity in our purpose, actions and decisions. It is easy to have a positive attitude to maintain a good quality of life. Value-based living makes us less likely to feel insecure and anxious when we experience challenging situations. Importantly, recovery works best when there is a willingness to change. Finding hope, developing self-esteem and resilience is easier when we follow value-based living.

95. In the present times, it seems very difficult in following a strictly moral life. Many deviate from this due to the fear of being left behind in the race to achieve success in life. How to arrive at a good decision regarding this?

Value-based living is a moral choice. It is about leading a life guided by values which reinforces self-belief and choosing right over wrong by true will and not by force or compulsion. Not everyone prefers to follow the same set of rules. Family upbringing, culture, education and life experiences play a crucial role in framing each one as a person. Sometimes, things might seem out of control and unfair. It is better to choose to be healthy instead of being right. It is important to learn to be calm in adverse situations, stand up for ourselves and know the right time to move on. The stronger we feel, the stronger we become. The most critical thing is to figure out what is really bothering and holding us back. It is good to voice out our opinions. Facing an issue will empower us and overpower the situation or circumstances that are controlling us. Learn to say "no" politely by sandwiching the 'no' response between two positive statements and briefly explain the reason for the disapproval. Have confidence in yourself, be clear regarding the consequences of the decision taken and stand by it. Try not to dwell on past actions by thinking if things could have been done differently or so.

96. Each one of us would have faced at least one major scenario in our life where it is a battle between values and the situation at hand. It indeed presents an ethical dilemma. Choosing to stick to the goodness in us, might drain us mentally. What can be done to deal with this kind of mental exhaustion?

Ethical dilemma is like a moral test. In order to pass this test, first and foremost it is important to know what is ethical and secondly abiding by ethics is akin to leading by example. We face ethical dilemmas in almost every aspect of life. Finding a right solution in such situations is very challenging. Analyse the situation or problem carefully, think of the outcome and choose the highest good possible or the lesser damaging alternative.

 **A BRIEF AID TO DEAL WITH DILEMMAS**

- **Voicing out opinion:** In today's world, voicing our opinion can sometimes damage our reputation. Hence, we should be clever enough to know when, where and with whom we share our opinion. However, holding our opinions back can be more damaging than spelling them out. Be mindful of the appropriate time and place to speak out your opinion. ☞

- **Avoid self-degradation:** Be bold enough to speak up and strongly disagree to be part of any unethical activity. It also indicates self-confidence. Never have doubt about the change. We might make a big difference. We might be the voice of our colleagues and society at large.
- **Analyse the situation:** By analysing the current situation, ups and downs, opportunities and challenges can be identified. This helps in working out, in the right direction.
- **Take the risk:** Living with fear stops us from taking risks. But taking risks help to learn and grow. It naturally boosts confidence. Always remember, failed risks are not always negative. Every experience in life is an opportunity to learn and grow.
- **Better Outcome:** When handling a challenging situation, in case a particular approach does not work, choose a solution that is good for most of the persons involved. It is the effort and intention that matters.

97. How to mould our children's thinking on such a foundation?

Moulding children in the right direction is the need of all times. This happens only through healthy and positive parenting. Parents always want the best for their children. It is possible only through a good parent-child relationship. It creates a strong base for their future and nurtures the physical, emotional and social development of the child. Being with children and giving them quality time helps them to establish trust within themselves and with others. Parenting is not only about teaching children "do's" and "don'ts". It is about making them realize their full potential. This is possible when we have a positive relationship with children.

BUILDING A GOOD FOUNDATION ENRICHED WITH VALUES

- **Teach children the importance of adjustment:** Adjustment seems to have no significance these days. Encourage children to be flexible when things don't work out accordingly. By doing so, it is easy to shift from limiting thought patterns to broad-minded approaches. Flexibility benefits children to lead a quality life with healthier outcomes. ☞

- **Be a role model:** Initially children learn more from parents. It is our responsibility to set an example by following values and performing actions. Whether it is anything big or small, they look up to parents and blindly follow. Children learn values simply by observing what parents do and come to conclusions that it is indeed the right way to do things. Consider a situation where we teach children to be honest but also encourage them to lie about their age to get a free entry or avail a ticket for cheaper rates to watch shows. From this, they assume that cheating is okay now and then.

- **Reinforce positive behaviour in children:** Recognise and appreciate when children share, be honest, complete their assigned work on time. By appreciating, good behaviour is indeed reinforced and they now learn that this behaviour is right. This works well in shaping children. Almost every day there will be at least one opportunity to teach and induce values in them. Use it appropriately. Talk and discuss about what they did right or wrong and how to make better decisions. Always praise children's efforts rather than the end results.

- **Teach children to assume responsibility:** Encourage them to complete the task they start even if it is tough and tiring. Stop them from taking the easy way out of challenges and teach them to take ownership of their actions. Let them know that if they break rules, there will be consequences irrespective of the triviality of the matter.

- **Encourage being helpful:** It is very important for the child to be empathetic to others' needs and it should start from helping out in the daily chores in the house. Please see to it that the chores are age-appropriate. Initially, work with them and show how it has to be done. This helps in developing pro-social behaviour. Pro-social behaviour contributes and plays a crucial role in individual success.

❑

Counselling

The Therapeutic Dialogue

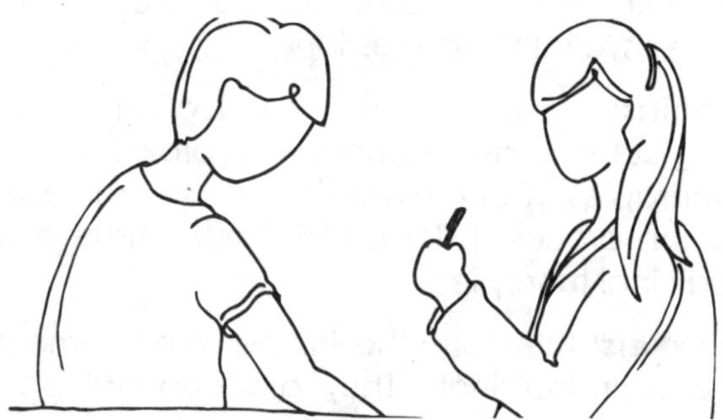

Expressing emotions and discussing about certain issues is a huge relief at times. Conversing with a psychologist in needy times is a therapy in itself, as they highlight different perspectives on viewing the situation and also assist by providing the best psychological support to tide over the crisis. Counselling sessions are most effective when one is receptive and willing to seek solutions.

98. We all have family and friends who counsel us during hard times. We also get suggestions to seek counselling services. What exactly does a counselling session involve?

Counselling is a process where an individual or family meet a trained counsellor to talk about issues they are facing in their lives and to find ways and means to deal with emotional issues. It is a safe and confidential environment, where a person can build a healthy and trusting relationship with the counsellor. The counsellor helps to address the problem in the best possible and positive way by providing clarity and also uncovering the root cause. The counsellor will help the client to develop their own understanding of the situation through self-awareness.

99. Who are the right people to seek help for mental health issues and for counselling?

Mental health care professionals will help deal with mental health issues. The role of each professional in the team is unique and each professional contributes to different aspects.

- **Psychiatrists:** Doctors specialized in detecting and treating mental health disorders. They will help alleviate symptoms of illness with help of medications and also can provide supportive psychotherapy sessions.
- **Psychologists:** Experts in conducting appropriate psychological assessments, providing varied psychotherapies. Counselling is an integral part of the consultation process followed by appropriate exercises or non-medicinal therapies.
- **Social workers:** They form the link between community and healthcare professionals. They are also trained in basic counselling services in poor resource settings.

100. Often many of them are averse to taking medicines for any issue. Can all mental health issues or problems be solved only by the psychologist with help of counselling?

Not all mental health issues or problems can be solved only by counselling. Each mental health illness also presents in a spectrum ranging from mild to very severe symptoms. In conditions with more severity like severe depression, schizophrenia, mania or severe mood disorders, initially the symptoms need to be treated with medications as the extreme symptoms need to be controlled and the mind has to function at least a little better to gain insight. Only then counselling will help in these cases, as a later part of the treatment plan. Cases with mild to moderate symptoms with individuals being aware of the issue but seeking help to overcome the problem, can improve only with counselling therapies. Individual's insight about the problem, a mindset to be able to grasp and follow instructions is necessary for counselling.

101. Who should seek help from mental health professionals?

Each condition has its own signs and symptoms. Most of them ignore mental health problems out of shame or fear. Any problem diagnosed early has its own benefits. So don't hesitate to seek professional help. Don't define yourself as weak or incompetent when seeking help.

Here are a few signs indicating the need for professional help:

- Inability to cope with day-to-day activities
- Sleep or appetite changes: High or low
- Loss of interest in activities previously enjoyed
- Social withdrawal and loneliness
- Mood swings
- Anger outbursts
- Decreased productivity in college/work and all other activities consistently
- Unusual behaviour
- Difficulty in adjusting to new circumstances/ environment/ situations
- Death of loved ones/ separation/ divorce
- Self-esteem difficulties
- Struggle with any other personal concerns
- **Suicidal thoughts Needs immediate attention**

Please note that one or two symptoms occasionally cannot predict mental illness. But it needs further evaluation if it is persistent and out of control.

Suicidal thoughts and tendencies need immediate attention from the psychiatrist. Extreme mood fluctuations and behavioural issues might need medications initially and need psychiatric intervention at the earliest.

102. What are the benefits of counselling?

- Counselling helps focus on the current problem and its future progression.
- Helps in developing well-adjusted coping skills
- Restructures the thought pattern with change in pessimistic thinking patterns to optimistic ones.
- Increases awareness on one's behaviour and influence of stress on emotional and behavioural responses.

❑

Reiki

The Healing Touch

Healing modalities are complementary therapies and have a positive effect on mental health. Reiki is a touch healing therapy which works on the energy level in the system. It provides relief in various mental health issues. It is simple, safe and effective. Trust and faith make any therapy do wonders.

103. Generally, many attribute mental health issues to negative or evil forces and resort to help from faith healers. Is there any such healing which helps?

Long held religious or superstitious beliefs are difficult to modify and in turn increase obsession about the belief system further. These beliefs lead most of us towards faith healers seeking solutions for mental health issues. Additionally, the stigma associated with seeking help from mental health professionals also make many rely more and more on faith healers. However, faith healing might have a short-term relief due to the faith and psychological feeling that it works. But the cause is not addressed. Many faith healers project their control on external factors and also impose a lot of conditions (rituals) which further increase the obstacles in recovery. It is not advisable to blindly seek help from faith healers who reinforce superstitious or religious beliefs.

However, many complementary healing techniques (Reiki, Pranic healing, Crystal healing, Theta healing) do provide relief in mental health issues. But choosing the appropriate healing technique from an authentic certified healer is very important. Any healing technique is authentic, if it gives the freedom to practice it flexibly.

104. How does any healing technique help mental health issues?

Healing techniques promote natural healing abilities by getting rid of all the accumulated stress in the body. It breaks repeated thought patterns and re-modifies it positively. This enables easy acceptance and moving towards solutions faster. Healing techniques enhance overall emotional well-being.

105. What is Reiki? How does it work on mental health issues?

Reiki is a complementary therapy which works on the energy body (pranamaya kosha) of an individual. It helps to remove self-limiting beliefs which cause the energy blocks in the system. Every living being is alive because of energy and everything around us also has energy. Mind is also active because of energy and anything we think once or multiple times has that magnitude of energy. By working on this energy body, all the aspects of mind which are energized will be altered positively.

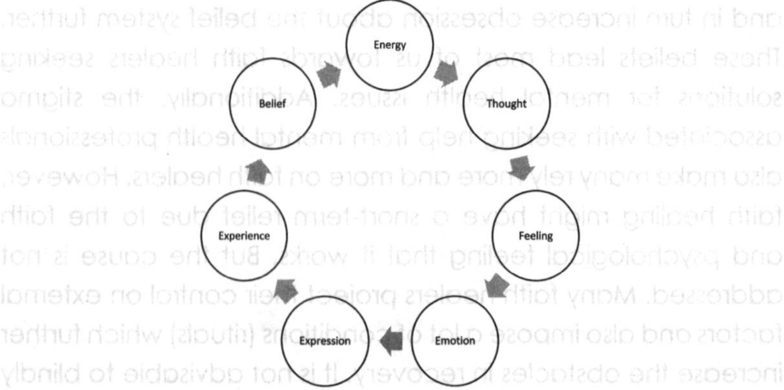

106. What are the mental health benefits of practicing Reiki?

Reiki has benefits in various areas of mental health. Some of the benefits are:

- Promotes positive thinking
- Reduces stress and anxiety
- Improves sleep
- Hastens recovery
- Emotional well-being
- Pain relief in chronic health conditions
- Healing effect on all dimensions of health: Physical, mental, intellectual, social and spiritual

107. What kind of mental health issues can be addressed by Reiki?

Reiki can address various mental health issues and also mental health aspects in chronic physical illnesses. Few of the common conditions are:

- Stress
- Anxiety
- Depression (mild to moderate with well managed symptoms)
- Mood disorders
- Eating disorders
- Personality disorders
- Sleep disorders

108. Usually, therapies have side effects. Is Reiki safe? Is there a risk of the condition getting worsened by doing Reiki?

Reiki is very safe and does not harm by either worsening the condition or giving rise to new issues.

❑

Appendix

A. CELEBRATE LIFE

Birthdays and anniversaries are often celebrated in a big way. Let us change the focus and celebrate a bigger blessing called LIFE. This is an activity to count the blessings and feel grateful.

Arrange for a small get together at home and prepare a favourite sweet dish as dessert for this special occasion. Each member of the family has to talk about at least three things they are grateful for in life. Thanks can be given even to persons who have made a difference in our lives. It will be very interesting as each one shares their view. After each of them has finished their turn, go ahead and celebrate it. Practice this every year as an annual celebration and see wonders unfolding.

REFLECTION TIME: Please note down the changes after the activity.

B. WHAT IS IN YOUR HAND?

Certain situations make us feel that everything has gone out of hand and there is no way out. The more anxious we get; we move away from solutions. This exercise comes in handy at such times and makes us aware of things that are under our control. Working on such things will change the entire scenario and we will feel empowered.

Close eyes, take a few deep breaths and relax. For a given situation, write down all the factors which are in your control on the palm in the picture below. Write down the factors not under control outside the palm in the circle. Work and focus more on the things written on the palm and notice the changes.

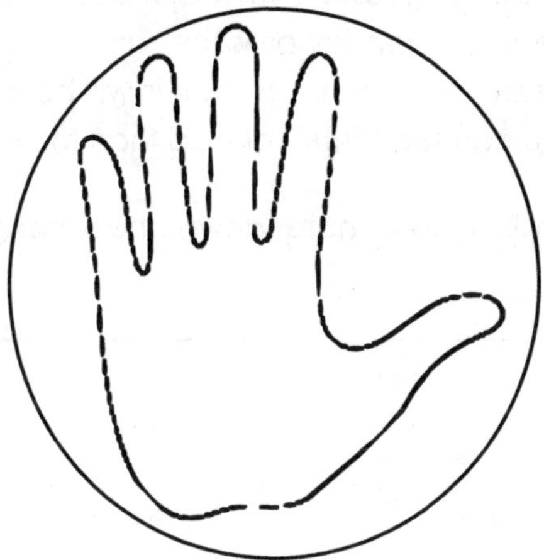

REFLECTION TIME: Please note down the changes after the activity.

C. LET'S STRETCH

Adaptability and flexibility are positive attributes which help us deal with challenges in a better manner. But most often it is our fixed mindset that inhibits us from being adaptive to situations as and when required. Everybody has the capacity to be flexible. It is just the thought patterns that need to be redirected. This small activity will bring a significant difference in addressing our fixed belief system.

Sit comfortably on a chair. Turn the head towards one side and note the farthest point you can see. Make sure that, it is the maximum point to which you can stretch. Now, close your eyes and give a gentle suggestion to the subconscious mind that you are flexible. Now turn towards the same side and note the farthest point that you can see now. It is will be very interesting to note that you can see farther ahead than the previous time.

REFLECTION TIME: Please note down the changes after the activity.

D. MANDALA ART

Art is a medium that helps one relax and rejuvenate. Art therapy aids in self-expression and gives an outlet for emotions. It brings a new perspective, relaxes and rejuvenates. Mandala art is being practised widely as an exercise for stress and anxiety. This is an activity that individuals of all age groups enjoy.

Choose colours of your choice and colour the different patterns in the picture below leisurely. Try drawing different patterns and creating your own mandala art.

REFLECTION TIME: Please note down the changes after the activity.

E. AFFIRMATIONS

Positive affirmations are statements that can help brighten the way you think and behave. When you tell them to yourself regularly or write them down in a journal, it can work because it has the ability to program your mind into believing the stated concept. This is because the mind does not know the difference between what is real and what is fantasy. Affirmations can be a powerful tool to help you change your mood, state of mind and manifest the change you desire in Life. But they work best if you first identify the unwholesome belief that is opposing them.

CHOOSING AFFIRMATIONS

- Affirmations must be firm defined statements
- It should be in the present tense. They should always speak what you are now.
- Repetition and frequency is important. Repetition plays a crucial role in building new habits. The two most powerful time slots to apply affirmations are the first thing in the morning and just before sleeping at night.
- Start off by prioritizing top 3 to 5 affirmations and focus on those.
- Affirmations are not a substitute for professional help.

LIST OF SOME AFFIRMATIONS

1. I receive love, compassion and understanding from my loved ones.
2. All is well in my world.
3. I love myself for who I am.
4. I treat myself with love and kindness.
5. I am very strong mentally and physically.
6. I live in the present.
7. I am a calm and positive person.
8. I feel calm and capable of handling anything that comes my way.
9. I am strong, confident and courageous.

10. I am safe. It is only a change.
11. I have family and friends who love me and care for me.
12. I feel comfortable expressing my feelings to the persons I love and who love me back.
13. I believe that I deserve happiness every day of my life.
14. Every day is a new day with new opportunities.
15. I deserve to be paid well for my skills.
16. I love myself and I accept the way I am.
17. I have unlimited power to bring good and positive change in my life.
18. I am beautiful, intelligent and full of life.
19. Nothing can stop me from achieving my dreams.
20. I attract wonderful things into my life.
21. I am whole and complete.
22. My contributions are valued and appreciated.
23. I am creative, strong, powerful, brave and inspired.
24. I am grounded, supported and deeply loved.
25. My ability to learn is improving every day.
26. I am excited to learn something new every day.
27. I believe in myself.
28. I have many who love and respect me.
29. My confidence grows when I step out of my comfort zone.
30. I am always happy and cheerful.
31. I have the power to make my dreams come true.
32. I surround myself with positive persons.
33. Everything works out for the best possible good.
34. This too shall pass.
35. I learn from my challenges and always find ways and means to overcome them.
36. Everything works out for the best possible good.

37. It is okay to say "NO" because those who matter don't mind and those who mind don't matter.
38. I fill my day with hope and face it with joy.
39. I welcome abundance of joy, love and money into my life.
40. I trust myself and trust the flow of life.
41. All that I need will come to me at the right time and at the right place.
42. The past has no power and no hold on me anymore.
43. I am willing to let go.
44. The power is within me. I learn from the past, live in the now and plan for the future.
45. I am abundant as money is constantly flowing into my life.
46. I attract financial abundance.
47. I am relaxed and allow my body to create perfect health.
48. I sleep soundly, deeply and I deserve good sleep.
49. I engage in work that impacts this world in a positive way.
50. I am willing to be kind to myself by forgiving them.
51. I let go of any judgements of myself.
52. I know what my body is feeling with ease and effortlessness.
53. I have what it takes to conquer my fear.
54. I create a beautiful relationship with my body and myself.
55. I live in the knowingness that my body's messages are important.

❑